# MIND & IMAGE

# MIND & IMAGE

## AN ESSAY ON ART & ARCHITECTURE

Herb Greene

The University Press of Kentucky

*Frontispiece:* Greene's Prairie House, 1962 (Julius Schulman)

Publication of this book was assisted by
the American Council of Learned Societies
under a grant from the Andrew W. Mellon Foundation.

ISBN: 0-8131-1323-7

Library of Congress Catalog Card Number: 74-18932

A statewide cooperative scholarly publishing agency
serving Berea College, Centre College of Kentucky,
Eastern Kentucky University, Georgetown College,
Kentucky Historical Society, Kentucky State University,
Morehead State University, Murray State University,
Northern Kentucky State College, Transylvania University,
University of Kentucky, University of Louisville, and
Western Kentucky University.

*Editorial and Sales Offices:* Lexington, Kentucky 40506

# CONTENTS

# LIST OF FIGURES

# ACKNOWLEDGMENTS

*This book might not have been undertaken at all without the exposure to architecture and art I received through the teaching of Bruce Goff at the University of Oklahoma. Goff's personal blend of pragmatism and aesthetic speculation together with his immense enjoyment of world architecture provided me with lasting encouragement.*

*My students have contributed to some of the design concepts that are presented in this book. This is particularly the case with the project for courtyard housing. Students have also encouraged me to assemble in book form ideas about images that we have debated together.*

*I also wish to acknowledge my indebtedness to Mary Greene for her help in clarifying the text and for suggesting a format that enabled me to submit a very diverse collection of themes and ideas to a publisher.*

# INTRODUCTION

In this book I use the term *image* to denote a form that acts as a symbol. Through images knowledge and feeling may be elicited from the human experience that has been stored away in the mind to be applied with new life in a new situation. To some extent any object serves as an image in that it can call forth a knowledge-feeling response, but an art image is constituted differently from other objects in that its sense data may be selected and arranged so that it arouses deep layers of awareness affording insights into our personal identity, our bonds with nature, and our communion with other men.

Images can also call forth hopeless feelings and dehumanizing thoughts. A society that proliferates monotonous housing, scatters technological debris, and replaces the natural environment with asphalt paving is surrounding itself with depressing images. Not a few life scientists are concerned about the effects on the human psyche of the increasingly denatured environment that threatens to engulf us. It is a hypothesis of this work that a healthy man-made environment requires the artful utilization of images not only to expand man's understanding of himself in the world but also to avoid the possible ill effects of monotonous and dehumanizing images.

While the subject of this book is images, the principal context is architecture. As an architect I subscribe to the principles of or-

ganic architecture and am occupied with the problems of constructing images that respond to the lived experience of the users of architecture. Organic architecture has usually been characterized as responsive to the specifics of site, climate, available technologies, and to the function of the building. It also uses as form determinants the social and psychological needs of those its structures are to serve. More difficult to apprehend, organic architecture draws upon the organic nature of life, represented above all by human sentience, emotion, and purpose, as these qualities manifest themselves in individual lives. The reflection of the life experience of the individual user of architecture and the expression of the organic nature of life are perhaps the least developed topics of organic architecture; they will be emphasized in this work.

My belief is that sense data that have become associated with the specific life experiences of users should be included in the man-made forms of their environment. When introduced as components of images, the data of familiar objects—their sounds, colors, shapes—enable individuals and social groups to participate more fully in their unique personal experience, in their cultural heritage, and in the organic basis of their existence.

The founding masters of organic architecture sometimes designed buildings that expressed the uniqueness of an individual or a social group. The Robie house, the Unity Temple, and certain other works by Frank Lloyd Wright may be cited as examples. But more often the masters were concerned with generic solutions to the house, the office building, and other building types. They rarely developed the possibilities of user experience as a determinant of architectural form. (The residential architecture of Bruce Goff represents an important exception.) A proposal of this book is that organic architecture should attempt the transfer of elements from the experience and consciousness of the user to the architectural forms of his environment. Images are considered as a principal means of facilitating the transfer.

Another proposal is that images based on life experience should provide an alternative to images based on machines. The growth of technology and a general blindness to the effects of images on the human psyche have contributed to the increasing production of environmental images rooted in the perceptual forms of technology. An architecture that responds to cultural, organic, and existential experiences can be a psychic bulwark against the misuse of technology and the trend toward mechanization.

While our thoughts and feelings are often affected by images, we are not always aware why a particular image evokes a particular response. In the first five sections of this book we consider the basic questions of how we perceive images and how images affect thought and feeling. My own approach to images in architecture is the focal point of the

remaining sections. Most of the illustrations are taken from my own work so that I can speak from personal experience, but I have also included the works of others where there are limited applications in my own work and where it is desirable to indicate contrasting points of view. In order to demonstrate a variety of perceptual characteristics, I have included illustrations from painting, photography, music, and other arts. These illustrations allow me to bring the subjects of humor, tragedy, and sentience into the discussion more pointedly than I could with architecture. However, all the illustrations have been selected to inform one another, and I hope that a meaningful mosaic will emerge.

Images are like organisms in that they are not made up of self-contained parts. Interaction among the parts is continuous and essential. For this reason it is difficult to imagine any sequence of topics that could mirror the transformation of images into meaning. The sequence of sections in this work derives from my sense of appropriateness in explaining my personal approach to images. It is not intended as a model for other investigations of images.

Finally, a study of images must acknowledge the difficulties of treating a subject the application of whose principles is so greatly affected by the student's particular background, outlook, and intentions. Undoubtedly, this work fails to recognize many of the risks inherent in the analysis of images. It is an exploration sustained by a naïve intuition and curiosity about the symbiotic relationship between images and the mind. Images are among man's primary means of communicating the seemingly ineffable—his concepts of life on earth and his feelings. The accumulated experiences of our lives, including our unique personal and cultural experience and the organic memories which reverberate from prehistoric time, are at every moment within us. Much of the richness of this experience, recorded and distilled into meaning by the feelings and intellectual activities of a lifetime, can be reached by an image presented at a given moment. The part of our stores of experience that habitual, socially useful patterns of attention and language have been devised to negotiate is only the tip of the iceberg. Images can help us reach and probe the obscured mass below.

# 1 DISMANTLED EXPERIENCE

*The past is hidden somewhere outside the realm, beyond the reach of intellect, in some material object (in the sensation which that material object will give us) which we do not suspect.*

Marcel Proust, *Swann's Way*

*Remembering is not re-excitation of innumerable, fixed, lifeless and fragmentary traces. It is an imaginative reconstruction, or construction, built out of the relation of our attitude towards a whole active mass of organized past reactions or experience, and to a little outstanding detail which commonly appears in image . . . form. It is thus hardly ever really exact, even in the most rudimentary cases of rote-recapitulation, and it is not at all important that it should be so.*

Sir Frederick Bartlett, *Remembering*

One value of an image is that its sense data can be arranged to bring about an awareness of experiences from other times and other places. Marcel Proust was one of the first artists to dwell on the power of a particular sense impression to release a sequence of experience from an individual's past. For Proust the important memories are not those we can recall at will but those that reside below our conscious awareness. Most of us are familiar with the way a sound, an odor, or some visual incident can produce vivid and often pleasant feelings without our conscious knowledge of where or in what circumstances we have experienced it before. At such times an intense consciousness of our being can result from the juxtaposition of the feelings attached to previous experience with the awareness of present existence. Proust felt that the revealed feelings could be used to recover the events that had fostered them. Sixty years later Proust's ideas were corroborated by the experiments of the Canadian neurosurgeon Wilder Penfield, who found that the mind records past events in detail, including feelings associated with these events. This memory record continues intact even after a subject's ability to recall it disappears. Direct stimulation of the brain by a weak electric current caused Penfield's patients to remember events, to the subtlest detail, that had happened twenty years earlier.[1] In addition, psychologists have found that present acts of perception often include the involuntary or unconscious recall of past experience.

The notion that the meanings attached to a sense cue can be rekindled when the sense cue appears in a new situation is basic to theories of perception and to the design of images. The complex feelings and high value associated with some art images result from the artist's ability to organize networks of sense cues to which previous meaningful experience has been attached. Le Corbusier's famous chapel at Ronchamp (fig. 1) provides an image whose overall appearance is not specifically like anything in past experience and yet possesses a diversity of visual cues associated with experiences valued throughout history. Some of the cues speak mainly of European civilization; others arise out of common human experience. The cues of massive, thick walls pierced by slits and small openings bring to mind Mediterranean buildings and European fortresses. Two of the vertical openings that reach from ground to roof are "blocked" by heavy, closely spaced concrete slabs (not shown in the illustration). Some of the form characteristics of these slabs and some of the feelings they produce are much like those of the grouped monoliths of Carnac and Stonehenge. The white towers of Ronchamp are particularly rich in symbolic reference. They are like nuns' hats and at the same time like the wind catchers of Tunisian architecture. The great roof, on the one hand seemingly without direct reference to past experience, on the other is vaguely like the heavy forms of such peasant artifacts as wooden shoes or the thatched roofs of farm buildings. Uplifting curves in the roof are like aspiring gestures.[2] Colored glass fills many small openings in the thick wall of the sanctuary, and the resulting colored light is a cue that often takes on religious meaning for those of many different cultural backgrounds.

The belief that meanings associated with a particular object can be made to recur in a new environment forms the basis of an approach to the design of images that will be developed in this book. A key to this approach is the recognition that an image encompasses a multiplicity of discernible sense cues, each capable of calling forth a multiplicity of stored experiences. The mind processes the sense cues attached to a present image by referring to the qualities of shapes, colors, timbres, odors, textures, and other sense data that are already stored in the mind. Meanings and feelings that are referenced to these data are among the stored experiences that may be called forth by the image.

Consider this example furnished by a television documentary on American folk music. The film opens with a pan shot of an Appalachian "hollow," a narrow mountain valley dotted by the small houses of the inhabitants. The accompanying music of the sound track was made by Highland Scottish bagpipes. As the camera moves slowly up the hollow, the sounds of the bagpipes merge with the sounds of fiddles playing Kentucky country music, producing an auditory montage. Gradually one realizes that the violins are reproducing the timbre of bagpipes. As the similarity becomes evident, one is made to feel an experiential link between the Appalachian mountaineers and their English and Scottish forebears. Thus a cue in an image can be associated with meanings that have been formed during previous experience and now are reconstituted in a fresh milieu. While the cue of timbre maintains valued links with the past, new content can be appropriated and symbolized by other cues in the image, such as rhythm, melody, or even a particular note played by a fiddle.

Arthur Koestler discusses the dismantled nature of stored experience and the manner in which sensory input is received. "The sensory input is screened, dismantled, reassembled, analyzed, interpreted, and stored along a variety of channels belonging to different hierarchies with different criteria of relevance. A tune can be stored stripped of timbre, and vice versa. The departicularization of experience in the process of memory-formation is compensated to some extent by the multiplicity of abstractive hierarchies which participate in the process, and by the retention of 'picture-strips'—vivid fragments of emotive or symbolic significance."[3]

In describing the process of remembering, Koestler quotes Sir Frederick Bartlett's definition: "It is an imaginative reconstruction, or construction, built out of the relation of our attitude towards a whole active mass of organized past reactions or experience, *and to a little outstanding detail which commonly appears in image or in language form*."[4] The

1. Le Corbusier's Notre Dame du Haut at Ronchamp, 1950-55

"little outstanding detail" which appears in image form (the timbre in the folk music example, for instance) may be considered a signal that can summon up previously developed harmonies of thought and feeling, but the interpretation of the experience that is recalled reflects the present attitude of the beholder. According to Koestler's theory, during changes that are normal to mental life new meanings and feelings may be attached to such a cue as the timbre of the folk music, while other meanings may atrophy through disuse. The memories left by past events undergo simplification and distortion or elaboration and enrichment as the pathways and schemata of stored experience are affected by incoming sensory experience.

In an image one can become aware, if only in a nominal way, of additions and alterations to previously established concepts and feelings. For instance, while one may recognize the large form extending beyond the walls of Ronchamp (fig. 1) as a roof, whose familiar meaning may be "the sheltering top part of a building," it is also possible for the beholder to integrate into this concept of a roof references to the shapes of heavy, thick objects, such as thick thatch. Curves that uplift or aspire, or those that have acoustical references in the sense that they make visual models of forms that control the direction of sound, might also be integrated in the roof concept. Additionally, the characteristics of shape that are European—perhaps French as opposed to English—may become a part of one's understanding of roofs. It is possible that some of

these meanings would constitute additions to previously established memories of roofs for the beholder.

An important aspect of the roof of Ronchamp is that its non-Euclidean shape seems to escape from familiar usages and associations into a realm that is mathematical, or free of any close ties with particular instances and objects. The importance of this "mathematical" characteristic of the roof of Ronchamp is that through it feelings of the particularities of roof, thatch, and the like are avoided. The powerful effect of the image is partly a result of the tensive contrasts between the recognition of established references, such as that of thatch, and recognition of the "mathematical" shapes, which do not seem particular. It is also suggested that the freedom from specific references within the perceptual form of the roof, as obtained by these mathematical elements, encourages us to become aware of changes in our concept of what a roof is. The mathematical elements provide an opportunity for abstraction which we use to reconstitute meaning.

Previously established meanings change because of the pressures of changes both within the environment and within the perceiving organism itself. We can see this happening in changes in the meanings of words as in our changing responses to particular architectural forms. Koestler notes that the aura of connotations surrounding a word in the mind of the person who uses it shifts over the years even though the dictionary definition may remain unchanged.[5] It is when

4

we feel an awareness of change that we become most conscious of our experience. It is difficult to remember our concept of the meaning of a specific word from ten years past, although we may be vaguely aware that it is different from our present concept. It is also difficult to remember our earlier concepts of *roof*, but when we look at the roof of Ronchamp, we can be made conscious both of a great many of our separate concepts of *roof* and of what has shaped them, because of the rather vast number of experiences that can be called up by the various cues arranged and stabilized in the image.

Images offer us unique opportunities to become aware of the ingredients, the complexities, and the changes in our concepts so that we can reflect upon their significance. With the stabilization of specific sense data in an image we can ask questions about the origins and relevancies of concepts and feelings that are associated with the data.

# 2 CONTEXT

*In nature we never see anything isolated, but everything in connection with something else which is before it, beside it, under it, and over it.*

Johann Wolfgang von Goethe, *Conversations with Eckerman*

*There are two ways of escaping our more or less automatized routines of thinking and behaving. The first, of course, is the plunge into dreaming or dream-like states, when the codes of rational thinking are suspended. The other way . . . is signalled by the spontaneous flash of insight which shows a familiar situation or event in a new light, and elicits a new response to it.*

Arthur Koestler, *The Act of Creation*

In order to be meaningful, sense cues must be embedded in a context that we can recognize from our stored experience. A cue is what we are focusing on, while the context is what influences our interpretation of a cue. In an image, as in most objects of perception, many cues and contexts interact freely. One cue becomes part of the context for another and any given part of the context may become a cue. For instance, when one looks at the palm of his hand, the fold lines in the palm can be a cue while the surrounding skin and outline of the hand act as context, or the outline may be focused upon while the remainder of the hand becomes part of the context.

But in reality the context of a perceptual situation is even more complex, including not only the physical surroundings of the object but also physical, mental, and emotional factors in the beholder. These latter factors lead to a tendency for the interests that are peculiar to an organism to control what it perceives. Psychological experiments show that human subjects who are hungry see more food objects in ink blots than subjects who have just finished dinner. The naturalist Konrad Lorenz found that baby geese, at a critical time just after hatching, follow the first large moving thing they see—normally their mother but in Lorenz's experiment, Lorenz. Compared to other animals, human beings demonstrate a very wide variety of contextual interpretations for similar stimuli. Consider possible meanings for the color yellow: a particular shade of yellow in certain emotional contexts suggests sunlight, joy, and refreshing lemons;

**Superwagon.**

2. Advertisement for Volkswagen *(Volkswagen of America)*

similar shades in different contexts suggest sickness or cowardice.

In our normal acts of perception we are blithely unconscious of the amount and complexity of learned experience that we use when we transcribe sense data into meaning. The Superbus image in figure 2 contains an arrangement of cues and contexts that call upon complex cross-classifications of experience involving the Volkswagen bus and the comic-strip character Superman. The perception of this image calls upon knowledge about spatial depth, flight, wheels, strength, bilateral symmetry, various anthropomorphisms, cars, comics, and a variety of other cues and contexts that could be cross-referenced in innumerable ways. But because of our particular contextual experience of the data, meanings are in fact cross-referenced only in certain ways. Certain references become contexts for comparison and evaluation of others. For instance, the thrusting "chesty" view of the bus is a reference to the large chest of Superman and suggests a context of strength and heroic deeds. No wheels are showing; so the bus is flying. Visual cues such as the skinny lines of chrome and the contexts of innocuousness and understatement provided by the Volkswagen aesthetic mesh neatly with the legend of Clark Kent and his steel-rimmed eyeglasses. The photograph of the bus, made with a wide-angle lens, creates an exaggeration of length and breadth that supports a sense of flying and power. Important in the original are the cues of color. The bumper has been covered with bright yellow tape and the circular Volkswagen emblem is red and yellow. These colors are, of course, those of Superman's suit.

The advertising program for Volkswagen has for years exploited the comic connotations of the VW shape and its lack of speed. A context of humor, made familiar by advertisers and a public who transformed the utilitarian VW into a beetle and a lovebug, becomes available for mingling with the humorous connotations of Superman as he sheds the clothes and demeanor of Clark Kent to leap over a twenty-story building.

The most obvious characteristic of the Superbus image is the commingling of the two figures, the bus and Superman, in self-consistent but customarily incompatible frames of reference. Both physical details, such as the skinny chrome trim and Clark Kent's steel-rimmed eyeglasses, and frames of reference, such as the unpretentiousness of the merely functional bus and the mild manner of Superman's alter ego, Clark Kent, intertwine in this process of commingling which Koestler calls a bisociative act. The device of commingling self-consistent but commonly incompatible objects or sets of circumstances was brought to notice by Eisenstein's use of montage in films. It has become one of the most widely used devices in the visual arts.

In the Volkswagen advertisement we find the bisociation amusing, but the device can produce many emotional effects and has one key function: it is an instrument for making meaning. It reveals a familiar situation in a fresh light, enabling it to elicit a new response. It connects familiar but separate experiences and directs the mind to conceive of one of these experiences in terms of the other. Through the process we become more conscious of our mental life and better acquainted with layers of the self that are usually out of our reach or difficult to recover.

Bisociation would seem to be an outgrowth of the more unconscious mental processes by which we differentiate sense data and synthesize them into meaning. An essential for bisociation is the mind's capacity to recognize differences and similarities among widely diverse experiences in widely diverse contexts. In the Volkswagen image, for instance, the curved contours of the bus are classified in the mind with certain experiences associated with a mighty chest, thrust, and the doing of work or deeds. These contexts are supplied by connotations of the Superbus symbol. The curves of the bus do not suggest possibilities that similar curves in other contexts could call to mind. For example, if the VW bus were superimposed upon a giant potato or a circus fat lady, other meanings would be elicited.

Bisociation is taking place when we look at the image of a building like Ronchamp and conceive of its roof as being similar to other forms in our experience. As noted earlier, the roof of Ronchamp may appear to us as particularly European or, more specifically, French. Possibly the most obvious factor in influencing our conception of the roof as French is the knowledge that Ronchamp is located in France. This knowledge can attune us to look for cues that correspond to our experience of other French forms. The roof in the context of the total image of Ronchamp suggests to this writer a boldness, a clarity of conception, and an all-out commitment to the expression of an idea that can also be seen in the structural eloquence of the cathedral at Amiens and in the bold gesture of the Eiffel Tower. The vivid contrast within the generous curve of the roof as it twists into a sharp point seems to communicate the notions of daring and clear purpose. The notion that the roof is bold, clear of purpose, and an uncompromising statement is in harmony with other expressions of the French character as it is often perceived. The writings of such French thinkers as Descartes and Pasteur, for instance, seem to me similarly bold, clear, and uncompromising. The French are also noted for many other characteristics, of course, but one value of an image is that it may include some referents and exclude others. An image, like Ronchamp, which includes contexts linking nation or region with valued characteristics of a culture can suggest a wealth of valued cultural experience.

The infinite variety of associative contexts allows us both to conceive of things (such as roofs or fiddle music) and to react to them in innumerable ways; but when we encounter these same things in an image, our concepts and feelings are focused and narrowed down by specific references in the cues and contexts of the image. In the roof of Ronchamp, in addition to the cues of shape we find cues of great thickness and of the pastoral. A cue of controlled but rough texture suggests the in-

elegant and homely. Together, these cues create an amorphous, but real, associative context linked to "things of farms and peasants." For some beholders the reference to peasants and the pastoral can touch harmonized layers of experience of great value, because man's closeness to the land is a deeply integrated human memory, no matter how little most of us care for tilling the soil today. The cue of uplifting curvature graduating to a point introduces the metaphor of an upward, aspiring gesture, so that aspiration becomes a context in the image. Acting as contexts, all these references and more are bisociated with the unique form of Ronchamp so that the meanings that we attach to them are gathered into one conception.

An image is built up of many discernible components. The image maker must organize the components so that they do not form merely an assemblage of unrelated bits. The organization depends on previously developed patterns of meaning of the most complex and subtle types and often provides an overview that serves as a context for interpretation of the components. The strength of the immediate experience of beholding an image depends on the availability in the stored experience of rich associations both with the details and with the overview. In Ronchamp, the roof is composed of details with rich associations. An overview embodied in the image of Ronchamp and believed by this writer to express a fresh model of constructing and perceiving images is discussed in section 24.

# 3 CODES, STRATEGIES, & MATRICES

*Seeing is believing, as the saying goes, but the reverse is also true: knowing is seeing. "Even the most elementary perceptions," wrote Bartlett, "have the character of inferential constructions."*

*The controls of a skilled activity generally function below the level of consciousness on which that activity takes place. The code is a hidden persuader.*

Arthur Koestler, *The Act of Creation*

We have seen that the meanings attached to a sense cue in one context can be recalled when the cue appears in a new context. Since more than one set of meanings can be attached to a sense cue, we must next ask how the new context can call up any one particular meaning. The answer seems to be in the patterns of familiar usages that are also among the stored experiences elicited during the perceptual event. Koestler refers to such patterns as sets of rules or *codes*.[1] Codes apply to motor as well as conceptual skills. There are codes for riding a bicycle, codes for winning at chess, codes for looking at sunsets, and codes for behavior in living rooms. Once mastered, the codes required to make coherent meanings and to carry out defined activities become largely unconscious. A code provides coherence of meaning but leaves sufficient freedom

for the selection of strategies to fit conditions in the precise context of a given situation. The adaptations one must make to ride a bicycle "no hands" form a particular strategy within a code.

Consider the response of an automobile driver when he sees a stop sign. Once mastered in terms of appropriate behavior in highway traffic, his behavioral strategies on the highway become automatic and normally remain unconscious. If, however, the driver is a young bachelor who has appropriated a stop sign as a decoration for his apartment, the apartment context will suggest to him new strategies for interpreting the sign.

The mind's ability to perceive the differences and similarities between a given perceptual act and a variety of past experiences permits visual cues to produce a complex branching reaction. The composition of cues in the perceptual event can stimulate an imaginative reconstruction of whole networks of organized past experience and trigger the memory of a far greater variety of experiences than is immediately suggested by the data in the image. Required for the process is, of course, the human appetite to make analogy in the quest of meaning. It should also be mentioned that experiences are cross-referenced in such a way that the same experience could be linked to many different networks of rule structures or codes. We have different codes, for instance, for experiencing a cathedral, a bachelor apartment, and a supermarket, but certain experiences might be common to all three.

For an illustration of how an image maker can direct the viewer's discernment of cues and his selection of codes and strategies for interpreting the cues, see figure 3, an advertisement for Pan American Airlines. The placement of the visual cues of the windows and nose of the plane encourages us to project anthropomorphic contexts into the plane through the bisociative process. The image makers have taken advantage of our coded experience that smiling eyes slant down at their outside corners. The plane window "eyes" and the curves of the painted bands directly underneath force recognition of the smile of the mouth. The circular nose with its pronounced highlight can be read as a "Mickey Mouse" nose. The highlight adds a reference of depth to a cartoon caricature that is otherwise rather flat. Once a third dimension is included, many more possibilities of meaning are revealed. Perhaps most important, the cue of the highlight combines with the disc of the nose to produce a sphere or globe. Since one message of the advertisement is the low price of flying around the world, this nose or globe becomes a multidirectional symbol whose diverse meanings can remain consistent although they are not commonly associated.

Smile. You're flying 'round the world for less than $1300.

3. Advertisement for Pan American Airlines
*(Pan American Airlines and J. Walter Thompson Advertising Agency)*

12

Artists have often designed subtle cues into images to which the viewer may respond without being consciously aware either of the cue or of the coded meanings that may be attached to the cues. The cues operate much like an Eat Popcorn sign flashed on a movie screen so briefly that the conscious mind is not aware of it. The practice of injecting subliminal stimuli into images that are utilized to sell products has met with substantial success as measured in increased sales.[2] The advertising men are only making a science out of what artists seem to have been aware of intuitively. Vermeer's famed picture of a lacemaker focuses on a young woman bent to her loom, her finger tips almost touching as she works a bobbin and thread. At the focal point a vertical joint appears between two smallish wood pieces of the loom. The joint is rendered as the shape of a needle, perfectly formed, and painted in black shadow. A few centimeters below the needle a horizontal molding on the loom which we know should be straight is subtly rendered with a curve that looks like a sine curve with diminishing pitch. Through the synesthetic experience that can result one almost hears a quiet whir of a rotating bobbin. And in Rembrandt's painting of Bathsheba (fig. 4), an image of male genitalia is subtly formed by the sheets of toweling directly under the hip of the nude. In this way Rembrandt provides a reference by which we can recover the theme of David's sexual intent, which is essential to the story of Bathsheba.

For the remainder of this work we need to borrow one more term from Koestler. He uses the term *matrix* to denote a pattern or assemblage of mental concepts that is governed by a code or set of rules. In figure 3 we can form a matrix involving the globe-nose. The matrix contains the knowledge and experience we have brought together from our experiences of "noses" and "globes," influenced by the context of the image, which sets the rules by which we form our concept of this perceptual event.

4. Rembrandt's *Bathsheba (Louvre)*

The term "matrix" may be applied to structures variously called "associative contexts," "frames of reference," and "mental sets," as well as to perceptual, cognitive, and motor skills. When a person looks at the famous photograph in figure 5, edited from a 1940 filmstrip of French troops marching to surrender in Marseilles, he may see it in terms of "Frenchman" or "European man," in response to the archetypal French or European face of the man; he may see it in terms of "Western businessman of 1940," influenced by the style of clothing; or he may see it simply in terms of grief of some penetrating type. Each of these frames of reference represents a matrix governed by a complex set of rules. A matrix is the complete store of data that goes into the realization, for instance, of a Western businessman, as it arises out of the limited data given in this particular image. The code governing the matrix "Western businessman" would be the set of rules established for the beholder by the cues of suit, tie, the face of the man, and the "city," made up of the woman and the building in the background.

Some codes are conscious, others are unconscious. Some unconscious codes may be axiomatic beliefs or prejudices. An example of a coded prejudice was offered when I used this illustration in a class discussion of the idea that cues given in sense objects influence thought and feeling. The students were to identify and verbalize concepts and feelings that were generated by the visual cues in the picture. One student insisted that his concep-

14                    5. Greene's *Collage with Weeping Frenchman*, 1961

tion of the grief conveyed by the weeping man was that of a man's selfish awareness of the imminent collapse of his business. The other students acknowledged that a man wearing a business suit could very well have been a businessman but argued that other cues in the picture created feelings that overwhelmed the "selfish grief of man losing business" concept. In other words, the majority of students recognized the "selfish grief" possibility, seemingly suggested by the cues of the pinstripe suit and the weeping, but these students used the flexible strategies of codes. They found strategies in "business suit" and "weeping" codes which were consistent with other cues in the image. One of these cues was in the posture of the man, stiffened in an attitude that implied pride and possible patriotism. It was also felt that the trembling of the mouth, combined with the data given by the eyes, contributed to an impression of vulnerability. The details of the eyes were felt to express grief, connected not so much with self-interest as with some sort of self-transcending ideal involving other people—"living, dead, or imagined," to use Koestler's phrase—as in a reverie of nationhood.

Other cues in the overall field of the image helped to overrule the "selfish grief" code. One was the face of the woman. She is apprehensive; she seems to be viewing something unsettling, perhaps awful. Her face is long, angular, and rather strong. Very important is her look of seriousness and the fact that she is not crying. These features set up dialectical comparisons with the round-faced, tearful, trembling man. The cues themselves reinforce the concept of disastrous grief while our attention is on the contrasts and incongruities presented. Our habitual man-woman codes governing weeping are caught in an inversion. This inversion, however, seems to touch layers of our experience that tell us the situation is real, that it is truly within the realm of natural possibility. Probably less important but still contributing data or cues that influence our interpretation of the image are the black clothes of the woman and the hard, somewhat ominous windows of the building. Together, the cues connect codes of experience that are capable of being harmonized within the matrix of the entire picture.[3] This is because many of the cues provide contexts that influence our interpretation of other cues—the black clothing, for example, contributes to the impression of "ominous" windows, which enhances the feeling of "grieved" and perhaps "fearful" faces.

Some of the interpretations held by the class members may have been inconsistent with the actual events in Marseilles; the dissenting student may have been historically correct in his analysis of "selfish grief."[4] We cannot in any strictly logical way prove him wrong. But it is important that, even allowing for cultural and semantic differences among the students, their responses to the cues in the image were quite similar, as in all likelihood were the responses of the editors who selected the picture for a prominent position in the *Life Picture History of World War II* (Chicago: Time Inc., 1950). On this basis, I would

15

conjecture that the picture is of emotional and intellectual interest because it enables us to participate in another person's self-transcendence and to contemplate experiences, real and imagined, held in common with other people, real or imagined. Matrices or frames of reference such as "grief" and "vulnerability," arising from the visual cues in the image, act to impose limitations on some of the other matrices invoked (e.g., "Frenchman" and "nationhood"). The buildup and interaction of rich matrices produce the uncommon strength of this perceptual experience.

To meditate on the facial expression of the Frenchman is to notice that practically all the feelings and knowledge of "grief," "Frenchman," and other frames of reference are recognized without the use of explicit verbalization. Both feelings and concepts are derived from complexes of harmonized past experiences on more or less unconscious levels. Our initial response to an image is seen to be largely the result of the mental processing of data according to the limits set by predigested codes and strategies of which we are rarely even aware.

# 4  SCHEMATA & DIALECTIC

*A dynamic comprehension of things is basic, for a correct understanding of art and of all art forms. In the replay of art this dialectic principle of dynamics is embodied in conflict.*

Sergei Mikhailovich Eisenstein, *Film Form*

Each group of scanning mechanisms of the eye and brain has developed to respond to a particular type of stimulus. Some mechanisms are sensitive to shapes, some to color, some to cues within the foveal image, and some to the field outside it. It is thought that the complete visual image of an object is really an assemblage of the responses of these separate mechanisms bonded together by the "glue . . . [of] meaning." Koestler refers to such assemblages as "aggregates of perceptual schemata, held together by conceptual links."[1]

Referring to drawings of elephants by patients suffering from aphasia, a mental disorder that impairs symbolic thought, Koestler shows that the visual image of the elephant "was not in fact a 'perceptual whole', but a melange of perceptual *and* conceptual entities; the glue that held the visual parts together was meaning. Thus in a number of drawings the tusks at first appeared on top of the elephants' heads as if they had been horns, and only when their function was remembered were they put in the correct place."

The mind organizes perceptual schemata in ways that are sometimes subtle and difficult to apprehend. In *Process and Reality*, his statement of the philosophy of organism, Whitehead approached the problem by abstracting shape characteristics from perceived objects and classifying the feelings produced in the beholder by these characteristics.[2] Such an isolation of the characteristics of shape enables us to focus on the process through which the mind, out of its vast experience, associates cues of shape with feelings and codifies their interconnections. For those who construct images the connection between shapes and feeling deserves study. The unpopularity of some of the shapes employed in architecture can be attributed partly to such a connection. The widespread hostility to the rectangular, boxlike buildings advocated by modern architects in the 1920s is probably a case in point.

To a considerable extent a beholder filters out certain sense cues and their schemata in order to concentrate on others. Thus the mind may filter out the particulars of shape to concentrate on the utilitarian connotations

of an object. But the important point about shape is, as Whitehead points out, that geometric forms can express far more than geometric truths.[3] A curve may flow, a sphere may be seen as swelling or compact, and a sharp angle may appear to pierce or move. Throughout history artists have, unconsciously or otherwise, produced precisely defined feeling in their works by using just those geometric cues that evoke the desired response. Tenth-century Hindu sculptors, for example, used bold but gentle outlines to project feelings of flowingness, sensuality, and ethereality into sculptured bodies (fig. 6). In forming rounded, swelling limbs they ignored the skeletal and muscular structure of the body in an attempt to express the world view that all things are pervaded by "one current of being"—a weightless mind stuff (sūksuma).[4] The rounded, flowing, swelling shapes supply frames of reference within which appropriate experience may be matched to the image.

Another example (fig. 7) illustrates the use of shapes in the walls and ceiling of a house to suggest a range of emotional and physical experiences. Among the experiences consciously suggested are aspiration, sensuality, power, and delicate control.

Since the turn of the century some artists have produced specific kinds of feeling in their work by organizing visual cues in modes that are radically different from those traditionally used. These artists' presentational schemes seem to refer explicitly to the dismantled nature of the experience stored in

18    6. Hindu figure from Khajuraho, India

the mind. They dramatize the fieldlike nature of perception, employing discrete visual cues that mingle and interact with one another. Picasso, for example, was famous for his ability to organize a relationship of cues in an assemblage, fragmented and rearranged from habitual and familiar contexts. It is as if he found that he could produce minglings and confrontations of matrices by using the visual cues of a familiar object, but rearranging them in the object with greater flexibility than would be permitted by the established codes of his contemporaries. Thus he might find it useful to make an image with an eye placed in some unusual position in the context of a face, or outside it entirely. A physical proportion, such as the distance between an eye and the edge of a face, would become a visual cue; once referred to one's proportional and contextual codes, it would elicit feeling in much the same way that characteristics of shape do.

It is clear that particular sensory cues, such as proportions or shapes, are meaningful to us because they call up concepts and feelings derived from our own life experiences. The particular experiences to which the cues refer often lie beyond our powers of recollection, but these experiences have built up codes of meaning upon which our daily experience is quite dependent. For instance, the feelings produced by the image of the popular cartoon character Snoopy are determined by proportions and referents that are acceptable to our codes and by familiar shapes that call up predictable conceptual responses. Our accep-

7. Interior of Greene's Cunningham house, 1965 *(Julius Shulman)*

8. Picasso's *The Dream*
*(From the collection of Mr. and Mrs. Victor W. Ganz)*

tance of the low-key zaniness of Snoopy is partly dependent upon the fact that within and even beyond a particular culture, certain meanings attached to proportional and contextual sets can be recognized by large numbers of people. Cartoonists and artists combine the visual cues in an image so as to call forth these nearly universal responses.

Culturally derived codes may gradually change with time, often through the observable influence of artists. Many people were not prepared for Picasso's distortions of the human face in 1915. Established cultural attitudes and codes concerning faces—to some extent still in effect—blocked the consideration of facial proportions as independent visual cues. An unfamiliar distance between an eye and an ear was not accepted as a cue to a wider set of experiences. The artist, however, paints an ear much smaller than life in order to utilize the feeling of the small ear as a component in the image. Through the process of cultural exposure, more and more people are able to respond to the intention of the distortion.

In figure 8 we see proportions used for their effect on feeling. In the lower half of the face, the distance between the eye and the thick black line dividing the face, or faces, is larger than life. This distance contributes to a feeling of bland amplitude that harmonizes with the large gentle curves of the figure and chair. The upper eye contributes to the image of sleep by being closed and by the cue of the "setting back of a horizon," which has connotations that can be harmonized with sleep.

20

The upper eye also provides contrasting feelings of tension by cutting entirely through the small area of the face in which it lies. Other cues reinforce the dreamlike connotations of the image: note the small breast that floats on the bodice and the design of the bodice that ambiguously suggests water or horizons. Picasso has rendered the face to combine two distinct sets of cues that can be read as contrasting sides of the human condition. In the context of the sleeping girl this device also helps communicate the idea of a dream-state.

The treatment of the human image to suggest more than one facet of the human being has a long history in art. A less obvious instance may be seen in figure 9. In the repetitive masks at the left, the large masks are read as visages, somewhat ominous and fierce. The eyes of the large mask, however, may be read as smaller visages with startlingly humorous characteristics. In this relief and in the sculpture of certain figurines, the Mayans were as decisive as Picasso in including two distinct facial expressions in the same image.

The different renderings of the two eyes in the Picasso portrait seem to create contexts to which we respond in dialectical fashion. An element such as the upper eye may be seen in the context of the face and the lower eye, and then in turn become a context to which the opposite eye responds. Each element of the successful art image emanates from the context in which it exists. The attention of the beholder shifts from one created element—accent, gestalt, rhythm—to another; whichever element one attends to carves out a con-

9. Governor's Palace at Uxmal, 1000 A.D.

21

text that is indispensable to its existence.[5]

A vivid illustration of the dialectic principle can be found in the rock opera *Jesus Christ Superstar*. This work also provides other analogies with Picasso's methods. An important example is to be seen in the manner in which caricature is used in the construction of the opera's dialectic system. Caricature does more than dramatize a satiric view or make something appear ludicrous; it compresses and exaggerates important gestalt-producing features. It can help produce an embodiment of an experience that is neither so abstract that the experience is lost nor so concrete that it provides unwanted detail. This is part of Picasso's accomplishment in his portrait.

In *Superstar* one is confronted with numerous caricatures. Pilate is worthy of a dissertation, but Caiaphas and the priests will serve as simpler examples here. Their low-register voices, grave, groveling, wheezing, remind one of the evil scientists on Saturday-morning television cartoons, combining into an orchestration of suspicion, calculation, smugness, nastiness, and portentousness. The difference between the priests and the evil scientists is found in the fineness of delineation, the rhythmic polyphony of the operatic voices, and, most important, in the contexts established by the story line of the opera. These contexts include feelings of the real conflicts and complexities in human nature, the real inertia of governments, apostles, and mobs, and a feeling of the impossible purity of Jesus' ideal. The play of finely caricatured priest-voices against these contexts causes the dialectical response that elevates the total complexity to the level of art.

An exciting technique found in the opera is the use of several separate cues to provide an expanding dialectical framework within a few moments of perception. A voice may express several facets of human character—jealousy, susceptibility to suffering, self-concern, detachment from ego—within the space of the same number of sentences by its own changing inflection and timbre, supported by the artful choice of words in the text. Each element becomes a context for the next. The artists carefully control the sequence and timing so that each gestalt element is perceived. It is not lost in a garble, nor is it too subtle to register. Both the operatic work and the Picasso portrait provide illustrations of the growth of human awareness of the dismantled character of stored experience. The images are treated quite openly as dialectical constructions of sensory cues within the interacting events of a perceptual field.

# 5 FEELING

*Art is the objectification of feeling, the difference between an emotion directly felt and one that is imaginatively grasped.*

*The artist is not a psychologist, interested in human motivation and behavior. He simply creates an image of that phase of events which only the organism wherein they occur ever knows.*

*The image serves two purposes in human culture. First, . . . it articulates our own life of feeling so that we become conscious of its intricate and subtle fabric. . . . Second, it shows that the basic forms of feeling are common to most people. At least within a culture, often far beyond it.*

Susanne K. Langer, *Mind: An Essay on Human Feeling*

In this book much is said about feeling—a response, conscious or unconscious, that culminates in awareness, altered sentiments, and affected emotional states and dispositions. In an image feelings can be symbolized by the artist. We can all recognize expressions of gaiety, sadness, or awe in images. An artist can stimulate a controlled range of feelings by his use of shapes, colors, and other elements to which particular feelings have been attached. However, most of our harmonized experience on which feeling is based remains unused unless there is a stimulus of interest, a disposition of visual cues and contexts that is out of the ordinary.

Rudolf Arnheim tells of a display of mangled old-fashioned clocks and watches in a small museum at Nagasaki.[1] All the clocks are stopped at 11:02. This image of a sudden end of time and the death of innocent daily action conveys a sense of immediacy. The watches dramatically serve as the sign of an event and evoke feelings connected with it. Although we may not have seen the clocks in Nagasaki for ourselves, even a verbal description enables us to share some of the feelings that are called up by the image. The mangled watches are only too successful in suggesting to us mangled bodies and a desolated civilization. The idea of time stopped at 11:02 can suggest the cessation of life, not only at Nagasaki, but on the earth itself. Thus, along with the poignant feelings resulting from our realization that tens of thousands of diverse and individual lives have been obliterated in an instant, there may be feelings of apprehension about the

10. Vermeer's *Girl in a Red Hat* (*National Gallery*)

future of mankind in an era of atomic wars. Other feelings might range from moral revulsion at being a member of a society that would use an atomic bomb on a civilian population to physical revulsion in reflexive response to the thought of an atomic blast.

An artist needs both imagination and a knowledge of feelings to create symbols suitable to his medium that will call up the feeling he is trying to express. We need to keep in mind, however, that in an art image we are witness to a created symbol of feeling, and not necessarily the artist's own experience of feeling. We must also acknowledge that the beholder who responds to a created symbol of feeling may not recognize the feeling that the artist intends to convey, for the symbol is subject to the individual interpretation of the beholder. Modern art has been the subject of famous controversies over the differences between the feeling intended by an artist and the feeling recognized by the beholder. Yet the fact that some images are deemed of great value, representing insights into human feelings that many beholders themselves would be powerless to express, would indicate that feelings can be projected into images and can be recognized. Furthermore, their stabilization in images is of great interest in human culture because of the insights thus offered into the attitudes and values of the individual who produced the image and of the age to which he belonged.

Cues in an image may awaken widely diverse thoughts and feelings, many of which concern essentially nonvisual concepts. Through the subtle use of visual cues and contexts artists have often seemed to evoke feelings by framing questions for the human consciousness, such as the "whither, where, who is she, what is her state of mind, what does it all mean?" questions suggested by Vermeer's *Girl in a Red Hat* (fig. 10). Such questions have continually been expressed in art images throughout history and seem, like archetypes, to issue from deep within the psyche. The questions are not themselves feelings, but they ask us to recognize and participate in the feelings which have been projected into the image by the artist. As examples of the masterful use of visual cues that involve us in subtle questions about states of mind and feeling, we will consider the Vermeer painting and the classic head of the *Mayan Maize God* (fig. 11). Both images evoke an awareness of sentience, the human ability for feeling or perceiving. In these images sentience is expressed both as a present attribute and as a potential capacity for feeling and thought not yet called into action. This acts as a context to heighten our interest in the "whither, where" questions and presents the beholder with a frame for thought that is open-ended, thus inviting his participation. At the same time each image supplies definite frames of reference, such as awe and notions of aristocracy or high station. For the moment, I would direct attention to the parted lips in each image as being among the prominent visual cues that express sentience. Often, parted lips are associated with adenoids and defi-

11. *Mayan Maize God*
*(Dumbarton Oaks Research Collection, Photo Phaidon Press)*

25

cient intelligence, yet the profundity of these two images remains.[2]

The mental process through which particular sense objects may evoke meaning has been prepared through the lifetime of the beholder. Lip data, for instance, have been referenced and stored in the mind in terms of contexts and possible strategies of interpretation on countless occasions. In the context of the art images under discussion, a matrix of sentience is synthesized with a "whither, where" matrix, especially in the Vermeer, where the eyes are focused on the viewer. In the Mayan head the downcast eyes without pupils contribute to the expression of impersonality and subjugation. A feeling of awe is communicated by the combination of elements of deity, sentience, and subjugation. The symbol "lips" as "the little outstanding detail" in an image, received concurrently with information from other cues, may cause the recall and reintegration of stored concepts far more complex than mere lips. For instance, the liquid, spacious, pearllike translucences in the Vermeer, together with the lips, may evoke unverbalized messages involving breath, limpidness, and a feeling of life itself. Characteristics of the girl's eyes form both contrasts and reinforcements for the sentience and "whither, where" matrices. She looks directly at the viewer, compelling his attention and expectancy with a certain aggressiveness. At the same time she is passive and not yet directed to action. Vermeer constructs a complex set of cues and contexts which mix attitudes and feelings in a delicately balanced composition. The qualitative aspects of the geometric forms (for example, the directional thrust of the hat, garment, and arm, which suggests action) are themselves ingredients in the matrix. Vermeer has imposed a pattern on experience that elicits an awareness of our own feelings about certain conditions of sentience, translucence, light, color, stillness, and motion—a combination of feelings that would be impossible to recognize without the medium of the image.

Proponents of organic theory have sometimes tried to show in their work how life and feeling have developed out of the basic units of energy that comprise all matter. Uniquely expressive of life, feeling, and energy is the freehand drawing by John Hurtig (fig. 12). A notable characteristic of the image is its projection of a figure that seems of monumental scale and yet also somehow alive. Tenderness, poise, power, and accommodation are expressed in an object containing cues of both animate and inanimate three-dimensional forms. The primary unit for the development of the image is a loop that sets up a rhythmic pattern suggesting energy, action, and growth. The loop itself suggests the scaly hides of certain creatures. Hints about the kinds of living things referred to in the image are supplied by shapes, gestures, and relationships that speak of the animal world but at the same time have links with human sympathy and understanding. The manner in which the enormous form accommodates itself to and sustains itself upon the land suggests the shap-

26

ing of architecture to the physical forms of a terrain of the kind seen in the work of Wright.

I have noted a variety of individual responses to this drawing. Some viewers have turned from the image with tears of sympathy; others turn from it in hostility or indifference. Certain connotations of the "creature" are repugnant to the intellect. Architectural allusions, such as the metallic details on the right "limb," may do violence to the codes of learned experience. For those whose strategies are flexible enough to accommodate the disturbing meanings, however, the image seems to objectify a rare combination of valued concepts and feelings.

For me the feelings most vividly evoked by this work are not easily expressed in words. They seem to combine poignancy, pity, and seemingly contradictory feelings of swelling power and helplessness. On the one hand the design expresses a welling up of life and emotions, reminding one of a great bird in a mating show; a supple skirt and armlike appendage are in symbiotic accommodation to the ground; the "head" seems to be making an amiable, tender, nodding gesture; delicate and perfect rhythms open and close along the surface of the object. But on the other hand the object, seemingly sentient and understanding, is blind; it is tied to the ground; it is primordial and undeveloped, like a great slug. These jarring contrasts, keenly distressing to the mind, produce an unusual matrix of poignant feelings.

I attempted to project a variety of feelings

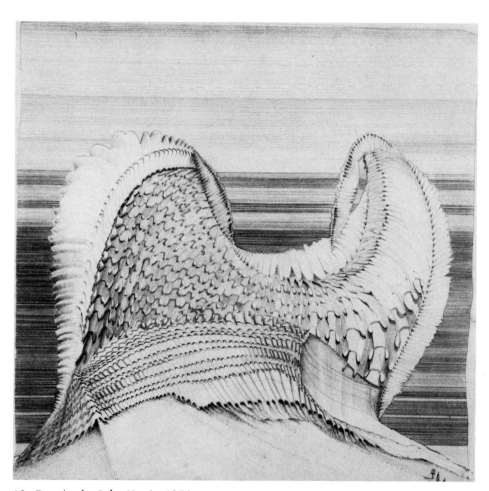

12. Drawing by John Hurtig, 1956

27

13. Greene's Prairie House, 1962 *(Bob Bowlby)*

14. Greene's Prairie House *(Doug Harris)*

28

into the Prairie House (frontispiece, figs. 13, 14). Awe is present, as inspired by the implacable and inhuman aspects of the universe. Feelings of pathos or tragedy arise out of the looming "wounded creature" look of the image. Suggestions of humor are afforded, mainly in the realization that the head of the creature is, after all, a man-made construction with intimations of comfort and shelter. In addition a feeling of protection is expressed by the sense of an enveloping coat and of a mother hen's "hovering-over," as well as by the cavelike interior. The soft textures, human scale, warm color, and lifelike rhythms contribute to a feeling that the house is in some way human.

One might ask why a feeling of awe should be projected into the image of a house. The vastness of the universe even to our limited perspective and understanding of this vastness is indeed awesome. I wanted to establish something of this feeling to contrast with the feelings aroused by what is known and under human control. In this house the image of a towering shape looming over one seems to evoke a feeling of awe. The Hindu temple in the form of a mandala evokes a similar feeling. Nearly symmetrical, it can be read as an anthropomorphic figure. It looms and seems portentous. In its presence one can feel subjugated as well as reverent.

In the Prairie House pathos is suggested by mixing cues of sharp and piercing forms with others that are soft and gentle, in the context of the wounded creature image. Again one can question the inclusion of connotations of

suffering in the image of a house, but pain is an inextricable part of human life. I wanted to juxtapose that which is vulnerable with that which is protective, sheltering, and comfortable.

In the Rembrandt painting *The Syndics of the Clothmakers' Guild* (fig. 15) the syndics are around a table. Their gaze and gestures are directed toward someone outside the picture, possibly a questioner. The arrangement of the figures in space suggests a grouping that includes the questioner. This grouping conveys

15. Rembrandt's *Syndics of the Clothmakers' Guild (Rijksmuseum)*

29

a balance that, with the support of other cues in the image, speaks of equality and democracy. Rembrandt demonstrated a unique genius in the construction of images to portray human character. In rendering human figures he often used geometric shapes to suggest traits of character and feelings about them. For instance, in the *Syndics*, the man who is rising has a sharp Van Dyke beard and a sharp nose. His collar and the peak of his hat are cropped. His fingers are pointed, as is his whole hand. Thus the entity of this man is infiltrated with feelings stimulated by our notions of that which is sharp, cropped, and pointed. In contrast, the seated figure, third from the left, has a broad face, broad collar, and broad sideburns. The seated figure second from the right seems gentler. His collar is curved, hanging long and graceful under sideburns that are also long and graceful. The cropped and sharp form sets in the context of the rising man and in the larger context of the entire painting evoke feelings of the cropped and sharp that enter into a matrix of concepts and feelings that we use in our response to the painting.

Rembrandt's arrangements of geometric shapes also indirectly help portray character through their reflection of human experience. An example is seen in the portrayal of the act of speech and the gesture of the broad-faced man. His hand is cupped in the direction of his body; the peak of his hat is elongated as if to further the notions of direction and extension, which are readily harmonized with an act of speech. The design of the man contributes to a convincing image of an individual projecting substance, directness, and equanimity in speech and intention.

When we look at the photograph in figure 16, we may feel slightly intimidated even though the sign in the background says Welcome. We may also feel the effects of an openness and honesty that we read into the face, overalls, weathered boards, gold teeth, and exposed fly button. Openness and honesty seem to contrast with authoritarian codes of "position above" and with the faint uneasiness we feel, perhaps because the hands of the man are not visible. A subtle tension is the result, and it arouses much of the interest in this picture.

A class at the University of Kentucky concluded that particular cues in the photograph cause a buildup of a particular complex of feelings. For instance, the jauntiness in the posture of the man, in the lines of his hat and collar, and in the flaps of his overalls is in harmony with the expression of the face and is reinforced by the position of the arm of the man who is out of the picture. The subordinate position of the viewer, who must look up at the scene, was felt to be unusually important. It establishes an attitude within the beholder qualifying his response to the events given in the picture. In the Rembrandt painting (fig. 15) the arrangement of the figures in the painting subtly encourages the beholder's feelings of participation in the event structure of the picture. On the other hand, our position of looking up at the Arkansas man sets us apart from the event structure of that scene.

We have already seen how ordinary objects or photographs can, like art images, focus our feelings and thus seem imbued with artistic values. The result is that a piece of "real" life becomes a symbol of the life of feeling. We are aware that the object is real, that the event in the photograph actually happened, that it is not a man-made image; and at the same time we are aware of feelings in imaginative response to much more than the physical reality of the object. This phenomenon is of major importance because it allows us to become aware of unexpected values that may be present in the perceptual events of everyday life. It can teach us to see with a new vision, and thus it can extend the aesthetic experience beyond the familiar categories of art images in traditional media.

Figures 17, 18, and 19 are details from collage paintings incorporating photographs. The paintings are intended to heighten particular feelings that seem to be objectified by the photographs. An attempt is made to merge the photograph with imaginative forms so that there is a suggestion of the mind's workings as it attributes meaning to the image. The painted forms are intended to suggest a continuum in which various components that contribute meaning to the image can appear.[3] For instance, in figure 17 there is a detail of vaguely identifiable wing or bodily limb hanging inert and straight down, located to the right of the man and just above him. The wing is meant to stimulate feelings that are compatible with those evoked by the

16. Photograph of Arkansas farmer by Ben Shahn *(Farm Security Administration)*

31

17. Greene's *Mixed Media Collage with Man and Bird,* 1966
*(Photograph of man, Dorothea Lange; photograph of bird, Emil Shulthess)*

photographs of the man and of the bird. A purpose of the continuum is to suggest that knowledge about gestalts such as the inert wing, and our feelings about them, stem from our experiences in other times and other places. The "unfinished" area to the right of the bird is meant to encourage the beholder literally to fill in the gaps of meaning in the thoughts aroused by the collage—to make analogies, suspend judgments, and dismiss incompatible meanings.

The beholder, of course, relies heavily on his previous frames of reference when he looks at an image. For instance, he may be disposed to seek a plausible story describing the relationships of man and bird. My own interest is not in making stories, but in showing inner connections between separate events by the association of these events with related kinds of shapes, capable of evoking related kinds of subjective experience. In this example the man seems piercing and defiant. There are signs that he has been worked physically; to say he has worked hard is insufficient. He seems weathered by time and adversity, but his back is straight. He is either defensive or attacking, somewhat like the bird. Other characteristics of the man seem birdlike: the sharp, incisive, down-turned mouth; the spray of ruffled hair; the pointed, linear shapes of underarm and pockets. The man's throat is like a buzzard's throat. One purpose of the collage is to encourage the beholder to look more closely at the features of objects in the photographs so that he can be aware of the cues that cause his feelings.

18. Greene's *Mixed Media Collage with Gandhi,* 1965 *(Photograph of Gandhi, Brian Brake)*

It has always been difficult, even for saints, to express spiritual love without having recourse to the symbols of physical love. The photograph in figure 18 shows adoring female relatives of Gandhi laughing over his remarks. The women are touchingly shown as at once delighted and shy. The rarest thing about the picture is the sense of cloudless happiness communicated by the facing woman. There is a communal touching of hands and bodies. The eyeglasses, white saris, and our knowledge of the life of Gandhi would seem to discourage a sensual interpretation. On the other hand, Gandhi is somehow worldly; he laughs and his eyes are ambiguous in expression. He leans on the women with a sense of the physical. His hand is on the neck of the woman on his left. We may be reminded of Gandhi's remark that he was making love when notified of his mother's death.

In the painting I have tried to create a passage expressive of a mixture of the spiritual and the physical. It suggests limbs of the body. Some of the forms can be read as the fabrics of saris or as forms that gesture and touch. The right end of the passage resolves into two forms that are vaguely like human figures. This passage is aimed at expressing the spiritual; but in the effort to suggest a spiritual love I have employed an element of sensuality that includes references to certain of love's physical forms.

33

19. Greene's *Mixed Media Collage with John Kennedy*, 1967
*(Photograph of Kennedy, Cecil Stoughton; photograph of marines, U.S. Office of War Information)*

Figure 19 is a detail from a collage incorporating a photograph of John Kennedy and his daughter Caroline. We are affected by a feeling of protective concern because of the protectedness of the child and the gentle touching of two human beings. The blanket heightens the feeling of protection. The straight posture of Kennedy's head suggests firmness. His gaze into the distance and Caroline's wistful expression communicate a sentience that is directed and yet suggestive of an indefinite nostalgia. Elements both tender and firm produce a sense of security that contrasts with our knowledge of the events of Kennedy's death. The clash can produce a feeling of poignant sorrow.

In the collage, the blanket is extended beyond the faces to suggest what may be called a continuum of the mind. The suggested continuum becomes a symbol of events and meanings that influence our response to the photograph, although these events and meanings are not explicitly expressed in the photograph and indeed extend to settings outside the photograph. Above Kennedy's head an ambiguous passage extending upward becomes a hand in response to the hand touching Caroline and in counterpoint to Kennedy's gaze that extends into the distance. The change of scale of the figures of marines supporting a wounded comrade amplifies a notion of distance. The appearance of distance is among cues that can involve us in a feeling of the passage of time.

Feelings that stem from our response to an image do so through a kind of mental shorthand, a processing of previously developed integrations of experience qualified by our attitudes and beliefs. While feelings are often of obscure origin, they are nonetheless a product of the mind. By our analysis of specific feelings and of their connections with images, we become aware of the record and the possible scope of our mental life.

# 6 CULTURAL CONTINUITY

*The bodies and the minds of individuals and the expressions of social life in the various cultures are the living records of the biological influences that have been constantly at work from the most distant past until the present time. Some of these influences have left their stamp on the genetic make-up of each individual person, others on the physical and mental characteristics he acquires during life, still others on his social structures. Humanity continues to grow by incarnating the past.*

René Dubos, *So Human an Animal*

It is a thesis of this work that images placed in appropriate contexts can call forth valued experiences stored in the mind. Those images with particular cultural significance may enable the consciousness to participate in the experiences, lived or imagined, of particular peoples. If an abrupt cessation of the use of cultural influences in man-made forms could take place, it would be an undesirable development, for the participation of the human consciousness in its history would be greatly limited.

Cultural experiences may be expressed in the groups of preferred proportions, timbres, shapes, and the like that provide elements of familiarity by which cultural continuity is maintained. At least until the most recent decades, artifacts and buildings have shown the impress of established, culturally derived codes, with or without the conscious intention of a designer. Medieval armor and the

aircraft of World War II, Volkswagens and Cadillacs—all show the impress of cultural codes in their proportions and contours. National and regional sets, or tendencies in arrangement and form, are sometimes the result of a complex of social and psychological outlooks. German scholarship, the "Nashville sound," and Eskimo art are alike in showing the influence of the stores of social and psychological experience that have been projected into them.

Salisbury Cathedral (fig. 20) is a building that produces a feeling that the psychological experience of a culture has been combined with an extensive historical perspective. This is partly because of the chronological span suggested by the variety of the statues of saints, columns derived from antique pediments, and early north European spires included in the sculptural details, but even more it is because these various details affectingly

communicate a cross section of human endeavors, whether ending in triumph or failure. This human evidence seems palpable on every stone—in the proportions that reflect human experiences, in the good or mediocre quality of the carving, and in a kind of happenstance sequence and arrangement of the details. The architecture is filled with a sense of human fragility that escapes the maudlin because it is bisociated with an aspiring and original Gothic form of overwhelming impact. We are given to feel that man can achieve self-transcending excellence even after primitive beginnings and false starts. While Amiens may be the great triumph of Gothic architecture from the standpoint of clarity and engineering—reflecting French logic and French values—Salisbury perhaps elicits the greater range of human feeling. The very untidiness, the inconsistency of the themes included, the sense of one element being added on to the next, and the reflection of a reluctance to be uncompromising are characteristics that are listed by the English historian Pevsner as composing a "national character that seems scarcely changed to this day."[1]

The valued attitudes and experiences that may be called up by designed objects in the environment are in peril of being obscured or even obliterated by our current attitudes toward technology. In most cases technology is given precedence over cultural and psychological codes, either for expediency and economy or for the achievement of the aesthetic aim of "purity" in design. Technology and economics have their own logic, but the

20. Salisbury Cathedral *(Anthony Miles Ltd.)*

psychological stability of the mind depends on a search for meaning. This fact complicates the notions of efficiency and economy.

It is in some ways comforting that even the greatest exponents of technological purity cannot entirely escape the influence of the culturally derived sets that have been programmed into their unconscious codes of proportions, shape, and form. Pier Luigi Nervi's dirigible hangars of the thirties possess characteristics that are not attributable to engineering formulas and structural theory alone. Some proportions and shapes in his hangars are as Italian in feeling as the marble sarcophagi supporting Michelangelo's famed figures on the Medici tombs. Yet Nervi is a preeminent figure among those who either seek to ignore cultural codes or attack their use as inimical or irrelevant to the aims of correct functional and structural expression.[2]

James Stirling is another architect whose stated aims follow prevailing theory but whose work contains images that extend beyond its circumscribed goals. Stirling's university dormitory Andrew Melville Hall (figs. 21, 22) on the coast of Scotland is a notable example of cultural continuity in English architecture. While Le Corbusier tends to detach a building from its site and Frank Lloyd Wright blends a structure with the ground by complex articulations, Stirling in some important respects accommodates the dormitory to the site and in others makes it independent. In taking this middle course he touches the traditions of English compromise, a principle in the architectural as well as the politi-

21. Interior of James Stirling's Andrew Melville Hall, 1968 *(Joseph Rykwert)*

39

22. Exterior of James Stirling's Andrew Melville Hall *(Tim Street-Porter)*

cal history of England, and adds English historical experience to the matrix of the architecture.

The building is formed so that each room has a view of the seacoast. The wings, extending toward the sea, shelter a community greensward. The glassy, greenhouse transparency of the public corridor evokes thoughts of Victorian glass architecture. It also sets up contrasts with the closed, sheltered spaces of the student rooms. The extensive transparency of the public spaces seems right for this northerly ocean shore; the cold, watery smoothness of the glass seems appropriate, as do the references to sea and sky that free vision offers.

Characteristic of Stirling's art is his handling of the windows of the dormitory rooms. Each room has two windows placed at room corners for both quality and balance of entering light. The view window is the larger. The grouping of the large window of one room with the small window of the adjoining room introduces an asymmetrical element into the repetitive, technologically expedient system of precast concrete wall units. The varied window sizes give cues of heights and positions that speak of human purposes and introduce a relaxing rhythm into the mechanically repetitive panels.

The plan and the expression of form and materials in the building also suggest certain political attitudes that are communicated by much modern architecture in Northern Europe and Scandinavia. Ideals of socialism are reflected in the private spaces that are qualitatively good but imply a uniform treatment of individuals. The separation of the public corridors from the private rooms is unequivocally expressed. While the building is carefully textured and has important contrasts in materials and form, one can detect a conservative attitude toward the kind of dramatic textures and contrasts in spaces that could provide a wider range of references for individual users.

Stirling's work seems to have an affinity with the technological images of ships, hangars, and factories. In the dormitory the roof promenade, parapets, and vent stacks are detailed to remind one of a ship. While the grey concrete, the long, severe outline, and the faceted form can be seen as a landform, or perhaps as a fortress, the ship references are more obvious in the cultural context of a political, literary, and lived experience filled with nautical implications. The metaphors of ships become resources by which the English users, in particular, can add complexity to their interactions with the building.

Unfortunately, modern societies have produced generally mediocre results from conscious endeavors to maintain ethnic and regional continuity in the environment—a colonial gasoline station in New England is the typical achievement. Such atavistic forms give a pragmatic credence to the stated views of the champions of the unqualified development of "pure" technology. This is the same kind of credence won by the school of Miës van der Rohe when it points to the existing chaos of the modern man-made environment

and then designates, as the rational alternative, its own symmetrical, insular prisms, detailed to give off a psychological image of technological certitude and Platonic purity. It is my view that most designers, including these great architects, fail to recognize the role of cultural codes as influences on their own design decisions. Miës, for instance, approached his building problem with codes derived from a classical inheritance that contemplates ideal form detached from a changing world. Miës's usual avoidance of nonrectangular forms—often of decided economic advantage, but, because of the visual tensions they produce, unsuited to the classical aesthetic—is an example of his use of a cultural code of which he seems not to have been aware.

Environmental design badly needs an outlook that would allow valued experience gathered through time to be injected into the new forms of a creative, changing present. Such an outlook admits the importance of coded psychological meanings developed during the lived experience of the organism. And in that it recognizes objects as assemblages of their aspects (shape, color, connotations of use, and the like), it permits manipulation of certain of these aspects to kindle continuity-enacting meanings. The bagpipe timbre of the violins playing Kentucky country music is an example of a probably unconscious manipulation to gain continuity. We need a conscious effort to identify and incorporate into the man-made portion of the environment the form sets that can help maintain our cultural continuity.

41

One way such continuity has traditionally been maintained is through the use of particular forms or objects that are culturally meaningful. In the artistic triumphs of Uxmal and other Mayan cities, assiduously repeated forms can be recognized as carriers of complex experience. The ancient Mayans translated the forms of an early wood architecture into the stone architecture of their classical period, as did the Greeks and other early peoples. The high, tapered thatched roof of the earliest Mayan hut was reflected in the great ornamented roof that dominated the classical Mayan temples. Also, small-scale representations of the early hut are seen on certain facades at Uxmal as recurring details of the sculptural relief.

It is hypothesized in this book that an object associated with the arena for the central experiences and acts of the individual may assume an importance much greater than its functional role justifies. Diverse matrices of experiences associated with the object, but difficult for the consciousness to recover, may be brought within reach when the object finds a context with appropriate reinforcing elements. The recurring huts in the Mayan reliefs are such objects; they call forth a feeling of communion with both past and future, a feeling of participation with the lives of kinsmen or tribesmen of whatever time. In some respects the value of an object to a culture is a measure of the valued experiences that can be attached to it. The process by which experience is attached to an object seems to be accumulative, like learning or growth. It takes

time for this process to be carried out, and, because of the complexity of the mechanisms involved, once a significant amount of valued experience has been associated with the object, it is not easily stripped away.

The modern viewer of an ancient city like Uxmal may ask how he is able to respond to the images of huts carved in stone, images that contain symbolic objects whose cultural reference has been lost along with the people who produced them. In viewing the images we respond to messages recognized by the codes of our sensory apparatus, an apparatus probably not appreciably different from the Mayans'. These messages are of human scale, rhythm, texture, proportion, and order. In addition our experience of earth and sky, mass and open space would find some phenomenal and existential agreement with theirs. By an act of imagination we can also surmise something of the social, psychological, and cosmological outlooks that produced the impressive networks of pyramids and courtyards. The Mayan builders' control of the experiences of sentience, rhythm, and mass can suggest concepts of the world and man's place in it. When the modern beholder perceives these suggestions, he may respond strongly.

When we alter features of the environment and reflect upon them, they can help us recall and negotiate the passage of our lived experience. Negative effects may be produced by some of these features, such as unreclaimed strip mines; but in the case of Uxmal, the features may offer a record of man's life of feeling. Images play an important role in stabilizing aesthetic values by synthesizing a record of sentient, organic life in objects to which the beholder's experiences can be attached. To sense our own life rhythms and our own sentience when we perceive an image is to have an enlivened concept of the objects we recognize in the image. Our cultural knowledge of the Mayan hut mingles with our own existential awareness when we recognize the sense of human life embodied in the image.

How ordinary objects become symbols of past experience is a topic to be considered more fully in section 17. Here I wish to stress that the art image is essential to the maintenance of continuity in human culture. I make a distinction between the art image and other objects. The art image allows us to participate in the experience attached to the image with more of our existential resources: a perceptually uninteresting Mayan shard may yield up the fact of its age to an archaeologist using comparative dating, but a vase in good condition can give us insight into what it meant for the maker to be human and alive.

One of the main functions of art has been to provide us with images in which valued existential feelings have been objectified. Bodily feelings[3] and the awareness of our own sentience and life rhythms, as distinct from feelings produced by what we have learned from others about culture and the human condition, are among these existential feelings. Our imaginative grasp of the existential feelings that have been stimulated by an image enables us to participate with an imagined consciousness of the era which produced the image.

In searching for an example that will more forcefully illustrate the importance of being conscious of one's existential life at the same time one is focusing on objects of cultural experience, I refer again to the rock opera *Jesus Christ Superstar*. As an element in the opera, the experience of bodily life is used to set up dialectical relations with a variety of our traditional beliefs about Jesus. For instance, the use of literal sobs and frantic "realistic" heartbeats creates an uncanny feeling of here-and-now, flesh-and-blood existence; and as the existential here-and-now is bisociated with elements derived from first-century Jerusalem, a nervous, exciting mingling occurs. Similar excitement arises when existential awareness is merged with other bits abstracted from Western culture, such as echoes of Handel's *Messiah*, the vulgar Cockney accent of a Roman soldier, or phrases taken from the contemporary business world.

Artists have always been interested in including actual fragments of the world within their constructions to produce a sense of immediacy and of nearness to the experiences associated with the fragment. The existential feeling produced by the sobs and heartbeat in *Superstar*, however, can seem unusually acute. These sounds penetrate the nervous system perhaps more irresistibly than the sight of the staged scene does, partly because the attention is not so free to wander during the sequence of perception in music as it is during visual perception, and partly because the created fragments of heartbeat and sobs resound against contexts of human nature, conduct, and beliefs that have deep roots in Western culture.

A fragment of the actual world effectively incorporated in an art image is capable of transmitting a sense of immediacy and reality without the distortion of caricature. A sense of nearness to the actuality of the fragment can be conveyed. This element of nearness may have been among the objectives of the Mayans at Uxmal when they used the literal image of the hut as a sculptural motif applied to their most sophisticated architecture.

An image that creates a feeling of shared experience may produce a response of intense emotion. This emotion is often rechanneled, absorbed, or dissipated by a chain of assimilatory acts within the viewer. Sometimes, however, an image can bring about a catharsis of emotion. During such an interaction between a beholder and an image, the beholder's mood plays an important part in determining strategies that give direction to thought and emotion. A related and perhaps less obvious fact is that a familiar object can act as a catalyst for the release of emotion that has been aroused by other events. Once the contexts and codes at work in an image have built up emotion, the human being actually seems to seek a familiar or meaningful object to facilitate the release of the emotion.

For an example of an image that for many brought about a catharsis of emotion, consider the ceremonies that followed the assassination of John Kennedy. The patterns of ceremony are very much like the patterns of an art image. They represent an attempt to channel the recollections of experience so as to elicit a directed response. The televised image of the funeral cortege slowly traversing Pennsylvania Avenue put before us objects that elicited complex responses partly directed by the mood of the beholder. We might go so far as to say his responses were partly directed by his need for an emotional catharsis. Prominent objects, rich in sensory and symbolic content, were available to the beholder. The objects could provoke various impulses in the observer, not all of them cathartic, but millions of Americans undoubtedly employed strategies by which the sense objects became focal points for the cathartic release of emotion. The white dome of the Capitol, the throttled-down sound of Air Force One, the horse-drawn catafalque—any or all could precipitate thought and feeling in an accumulative and directed manner. It is doubtful that the sight of some other nation's capitol, for example, could have ignited as sympathetic a response as did the white dome on Pennsylvania Avenue in the context of the Kennedy funeral.

The recurrence of forms in art and architecture and their gradual evolution throughout the generations of a culture suggest that one use of form is to provide a sense of nearness to the past through the evocation of shared experiences that are meaningful to the culture. It is evident, however, that modern attempts to perpetuate symbols of the past in architecture or artifacts are often debased. The subdivision of period houses, more surreal than a Dali limp-watch landscape, is an example of the type that prompts progressives to denounce overt symbols of the past used in attempts to assuage the desire for cultural continuity. Yet the importance of psychological continuity and cultural identity cannot escape us as evidence mounts that many recent technologically adequate environments are producing human alienation.

# 7 TIME & TIMELESSNESS

*The aesthetic experience depends on that delicate balance arising from both matrices in the mind: on perceiving the hero as Laurence Olivier and Prince Hamlet of Denmark at one and the same time; on the lightning between charged electrodes. It is this precarious suspension of awareness between the two planes which facilitates the continuous flux of emotion from the Now and Here to the remoter worlds of the Then and There, and the cathartic effects resulting from it. For when interest is deflected from the self it will attach itself to something else; when the level of self-assertive tension falls, the self-transcending impulses become almost automatically dominant. Thus the creation of illusion is in itself of cathartic value.*

Arthur Koestler, *The Act of Creation*

We often use the word timeless to describe images. Possibly we use it most frequently to characterize a valued expression or quality in an image that does not seem tied to any particular time or place. Awareness of the passage of time and anticipation of the future are ingredients in some of the most affecting of human realizations; the consciousness of timelessness—that is, of feelings that seem to transcend the time in which an image was made—is one of the impressive effects of images.

Various qualities in the image and attitudes in the beholder can both trigger a valued recognition of time as past, present, or future and suspend time from apparent connection to these realities. While the subject of the projection of time into images is difficult to grasp, the role of time and timelessness as valued reference frames is important, and this prompts me to offer some tentative observations about their nature.

In one sense the successful art image of any period tends to effect a realization of both time and timelessness in that the viewer becomes conscious of more than one period of time. One time set is suggested by the viewer's realization of the period the image represents or suggests. Generally this realization is a response to the subject, the medium in which the image is rendered, and the style, all of which tend to place the work in a specified framework of time, whether the age of Cro-Magnon man or the twentieth century. Another time set arises out of the awareness of the "Now and Here," the present moment.

23. Greene's *Collage with Seated Woman*, 1962
*(Photograph of woman, Henri Cartier-Bresson)*

This awareness results from the lifelike qualities of the image which stir the viewer's sense of being alive. Such a response enables him to empathize with the image and involve his own life as part of this response. Thus a sense of the immediacy of the viewer's own life becomes a component in the image at the same time he is aware of realizations about the period or periods suggested by the image.

Cartier-Bresson's photograph of a lady on a park bench (fig. 23), in addition to involving us in this kind of awareness of two different times, provides a symbol of the human consciousness in contemplation of time. The photograph of the real person on the bench becomes a particularly enriched symbol of the human capability for self-reflection because of the powerfully harmonized references of dreamy introspection, suspension in space, flow through space, age, and feminine personality that the photographer has miraculously captured.

The ancient city of Uxmal (fig. 9) provides another kind of example. The proportional set that enabled the Mayan to participate in his past, the pyramid that becomes at once an altar and a visible model of societal effort, the familiar object of the hut of peasants and kings, the human scale—all these provide elements of matrices that facilitate the transfer of attention from the Now and Here to the Then and There. Attention may be directed toward other persons, real or imagined, or perhaps to forms of nature such as mountains or plains.

An object, such as the Mayan hut, that is

48

able to awaken the recognition of time-spanning experience can be a vehicle for interaction between the Now and Here and the Then and There. While any object, even a shard or a grain of sand, can spark some degree of interaction if the intellect so chooses, certain objects and contexts can evoke unusually rich responses of this kind. It appears that only when appropriate symbols and contexts express valued life experiences do the deeper realizations of time occur.

If such experiences were not difficult to reclaim, then we would not feel their value when we recognize them in an image. The rarity we sense in looking at a Vermeer is based not so much on the knowledge that Vermeer produced fewer than thirty pictures, and these of diminutive size, as on the rare combination of feelings that we recognize in his images, such as the indefinite nostalgia coexisting with a feeling that mind is being concretized in the matter that constitutes the sunlight, milk pitchers, and human figures in his paintings. There is the feeling that time itself is frozen at an instant, which Vermeer created to a degree perhaps unsurpassed by any other artist. We recognize such feelings even though their origins and causes seem either a mystery or beyond the power of verbal expression.

The deepest emotional basis for our feelings about time probably lies in our awareness of the course of our lives and in our ultimate uncertainty about where we came from and where we are going. This existential substrate makes time most real to us and makes us susceptible to symbols, such as the lady in Cartier-Bresson's photograph and Vermeer's *Girl in a Red Hat*, that can bring an acute consciousness of our condition. Both of these works, by involving us in this substrate and in other strong reference frames already mentioned, provoke unusually deep realizations of both time and timelessness.

In designing the Prairie House (frontispiece, figs. 13, 14), I made a conscious attempt to evoke a sense of time by including in the image a range of references that span the ages from the primordial past to an intimated distant future. Metaphors of beast and cave are included, along with suggestions of the biological world and of technological objects of the future. These contrasting images are combined with the image of "vibratory" activity (established by the rhythms of boards and shingles) to suggest that the diverse metaphors and references to different times are actively involved in the present image.[1]

The design of the Prairie House was intended to achieve the reverse of the classical objectives of resolving tensions and resisting the impress of time and change. I wanted to create the impression that the diversities of experience gathered under the symbols of roof, shelter, coat, creature, and futurist object are seen as details actively entering into a realization of "house" during an act of consciousness. The design represents an attempt at a poetic rendering of many meanings and fringe connotations simultaneously.[2] The concrete expression of the total meaning of an object

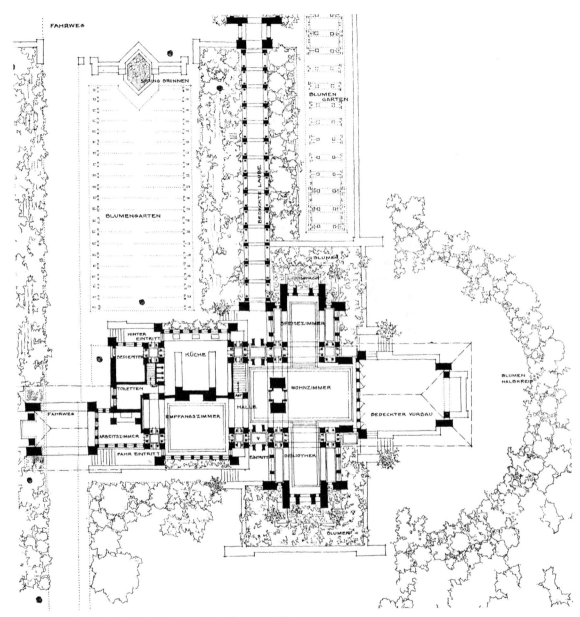

FAHRWEG

SPRING BRUNNEN

BLUMEN GARTEN

BEDECKTE LAUBE

BLUMENGARTEN

BLUMEN

LICHTSCHACHT

SPEISEZIMMER

HINTER EINTRITT

BEDIENTEN

KÜCHE

BLUMEN HALBKREIS

WOHNZIMMER

TOILETTEN

HALLE

BEDECKTER VORBAU

EMPFANGSZIMMER

FAHRWEG

ARBEITSZIMMER

FAHR EINTRITT

EINTRITT

BIBLIOTHEK

BLUMEN

24. Plan of Frank Lloyd Wright's Martin house, 1904

requires reference to diverse orders of things whose occurrences are distributed through time. The image of the Prairie House represents an attempt to demonstrate the process of concrete expression as an object itself for our imaginative contemplation.

Another way of looking at the problem of time and timelessness in an image is to consider the more abstract pattern of its design. In a successful work of art, the pattern of the whole conveys a feeling that essential relationships exist between the data in the image and the world beyond the image. The result is a feeling that there is something important to be unraveled in the manner in which the pattern in the image is connected to the world. I first felt the force of this idea while studying the floor plans of Frank Lloyd Wright. The plan of the Martin house (fig. 24) can be enjoyed as a two-dimensional composition irrespective of its function as a floor plan. Wright must have felt this, because he had the plan rendered to dramatize its compositional values. The composition displays balance, gradation, terminals, interpenetration, and other valued elements. The beholder responds because of his lifetime of experience with these elements. The pattern appears as an idealization of relationships and elements derived from the world of times and places beyond the present pattern.

Our awareness of experience on two simultaneous levels is also strong when we are in the presence of the actual built spaces of Wright's architecture. We feel the space with our immediate awareness of its characteristics of shelter, variegated light, harmoniously combined materials, and spatial extensions that lead the eye beyond the perceived space. The awareness places us fully in the Now and Here. At the same time, Wright's composition calls up an awareness of an idealized pattern that represents an important understanding of a Then and There world beyond the presently perceived space. An emotional and intellectual response accompanies this awareness of an idealized time (past, present, or future) involving itself in the Now and Here.

The comprehension of any perceived object requires a thought process that mixes past experience with the present event, but it is the art image that can present an idealized pattern. In our perception of the idealized pattern, our awareness of the relationships and references represented in the image is heightened. We are aware that we are experiencing a valued coordination of the occurrences of different times and different places. Such an awareness can be preverbal, manifesting itself simply as a feeling of the importance of the image. And we may be unconscious of some of the references of the pattern. The Martin house embodies a pattern that is relatively easy to identify so that one can talk about some of its aspects. In the Vermeer painting (fig. 10), on the other hand, the pattern of significance is just as active; but it is so subtle and miraculously diffused that one is at a loss to identify its characteristics, though the feeling it creates can be very intense. At any rate, it is in general the interesting combination of references to the Now and Here with references to the world of time past or future or to the realm of significant abstract thought that produces the feeling of the timeless in images. The beholder responds to the image with the immediate experience of his own life at the same time that he responds to the idealized pattern that refers to the world of other times and other places.

# 8 OPEN-ENDEDNESS & COMPLEXITY

*It seems to me that there should be only allusions. The contemplation of objects, the volatile image of dreams they evoke, these make the song: the Parnassians who make a complete demonstration of the object thereby lack mystery.*

Stéphane Mallarmé, *Enquête sur l'évolution littèraire*

A concept of great importance in a discussion of images and the complexity of experience is open-endedness, or a quality of indefinitely expansible possibilities. Turner's paintings offer exceptionally clear-cut examples of the use of this concept. Turner was interested in making explicit references to such recognizable objects as clouds and cliffs by means of elements that seem also to refer to other things. In his works, crystalline facets, tiny lines, and shimmering eddies that are seemingly without form are shaped into intense, information-giving constructs of landform, ship, sky, light, or water. They also suggest a multitude of undetermined things that can stir us to higher levels of imagination.

In Turner's *Burial at Sea* (fig. 25) the hull of the ship lacks definite boundaries. The black ship merges with its black reflection and the intersection of deck and sky is blurred. The presence of ship paraphernalia is intimated, although practically no explicit detail is given. Probably the definiteness of pairs of inky black sails against the sky gives more "ship" information initially than does the hazy rendering of the hull. The large divisions of the hull count as units but are subject to vague possibilities of further division. These indefinite possibilities make the image open-ended for the beholder. The inclusion of the multiplicities within the gestalt closure of the hull and its uniform black rendering are important. The notions of *hull* and *blackness* impose limitations, or reduce the range of the types of indefiniteness, by providing associative contexts and frames of reference. The vertical passage of light that starts on the ship and continues to the bottom of the picture is another open-ended system in the painting. The fiery light is harmonized with the ship by qualitative likenesses and a similar handling of vagueness and clarity.

The image sets up a tension between notions of vagueness and of clarity. It is the meeting and reconciliation of these within the frames of reference of ship, sea, blackness,

25. Turner's *Peace: Burial at Sea* (Tate Gallery)

and light that hold the attention of the beholder. It should be noted that very little of this process, which includes a transfer of attention from the "Now and Here" of the ship-fire to the "Then and There" of its indefinite possibilities, takes place on verbal levels of consciousness. It should also be noted that the "Then and There" may refer to indefinite possibilities of the future as well as the past.

The architect whose spatial constructs offer the closest analogy to the open-endedness found in this Turner picture is Frank Lloyd Wright. Employing a similar accumulation of many related parts, he achieves a feeling of unending space in his buildings. The plan of the Martin house (fig. 24) illustrates how clearly Wright conceived of an open-ended space. A person standing at the intersection of the corridor axes near the fireplace in the living room would not see a definite limiting wall, but instead would look through a space that seems to emerge from the three-dimensional complex of piers, planes, and grilles. Acting as limitations are the associative contexts imposed by these various features. The colors and textures of their materials, gradients of light, sheltering roof, and the great hearth are seen in a spatial medium without end. The space within and just out of sight seems charged with interest lent by the features; yet because of the sense of expectancy elicited by the space, the beholder seems to be asked to supplement the possibilities of interpretation with his own experience.

The creation of open-ended constructs is a

poetic response to the task of organizing innumerable experiences. Photography and film-making, as practiced by artists, have shown that a poetic perception of actual events is very close to, or perhaps the same as, the construct of events that is an art image. Each presents harmonized experience in a framework that possesses the possibilities of both clarity and vagueness. The photographer Cartier-Bresson is particularly able to recognize in an instant this type of framework in an actual event. The extraordinary example of his work shown in figure 23 demonstrates the interest of open-endedness for the human consciousness.

The dreaming, rapt face in the context of other cues suggests a reverie. The attenuated figure seems to float as if suspended in space and time. The streaming, linear motion of the slat bench evokes a feeling of space and time extending into the distance. The dramatic angle of perspective is in powerful counterpoint to the dreaming reverie established by the face; the straightness of the figure also sets up a counterpoint with the extending slat bench. The definiteness of hat, negligee, profile, clutch of hands, newspaper, bench, and cane gives explicit resources with which the beholder can pin down his experience and feeling against reference frames of indefinite dreaming and the vagueness of extension into space and time.

The power of the photograph stems from the vivid way that reverie, a long life, and space and time are dramatized as primary contexts, rich with open-ended possibilities of interpretation. The hat, the newspaper, the cane, and other details might well have been somewhat different and we could probably still have accommodated them within the flexible strategies of codes suggested by the primary contexts. The importance of open-endedness in an image seems to lie in the intensity and direction of the participatory modes it allows the beholder and in the manner in which they can be combined.

Rapoport and Kantor discuss open-endedness as one type of stimulus acting to increase the complexity that a person is able to cope with and enjoy at a given moment.[1] It allows the beholder to use a small amount of detail in an object or in an image to build a mental matrix that includes experiences outside and beyond what he sees. This forms a "background of meaning" for the object while at the same time infusing the experience of viewing it with an open-ended character. The percipient is encouraged to develop higher thresholds of complexity by the incentive of curiosity which is supplied by the ambiguous or open-ended aspects of the stimulus and their inferred meanings.

Psychologists have studied the effects of ambiguity and complexity on human and animal subjects. Various investigations of the thresholds of boredom, confusion, enjoyment, and curiosity encountered during the process of learning to perform tasks show that the search for stimulus-variability and complexity is a fundamental incentive. Rapoport and Kantor cite this evidence to support their thesis that open-endedness, complexity, and allusiveness in building are more psychologically satisfying than the traditional simplicity sought by many designers. These authors make a case for the values of ambiguity, which they define as any nuance, however slight, that encourages alternate reactions to the same building or building group.

We may postulate that the possibility of alternate interpretations within some known framework, whether the framework is the outline of a building, the image of a ship, or a test maze for white mice, may be a prerequisite to the avoidance of perceptual boredom. Art images attest that some people have known this or at least suspected it for ages, but perhaps the authority of science can spread the idea to institutions such as governmental housing bureaus, which, the world over, are encouraging the production of some of the most unambiguous environments in history. In addition a scientific examination of the subject of environmental complexity might be able to offer useful data for designers who are trying to determine the type and amount of complexity appropriate to particular design situations.

A design project that employs open-endedness on an intuitive level is the theater illustrated in figures 26 and 27. The project, dating from 1962, is for an arena theater. The theater space is spanned by great trusses, which support a scaffold over the entire house. The scaffold provides access to stage lights and to manually adjustable acoustic baffles, as well as making overhead staging practical. It also accommodates set storage within the depth of the structure. Horizontally the trusses extend well beyond the audience. In depth they range from thirteen feet in the section over the audience to twenty-six feet over the stage.

In addition to their functional value, the trusses have visual characteristics that could be utilized by the audience as devices to make meaning. With proper lighting the trusses could form an open-ended perceptual space, dissolving the definite ceiling plane into a space of indefinite limits. The effect would be rather like a view into a forest. The design aim was to create a multiplicity of members with possibilities for suggesting things beyond the events depicted on the stage. In an all-purpose theater, undefined or at least ambiguous elements are considered to form a potentially useful background, from which the beholder can derive alternative meanings appropriate to various stagings and performances. It is also felt to be important that the physical forms defining the space remain rather anonymous—that is, that they not carry too obviously the messages and time sets of particular architectural styles. For a civic theater given over to a wide range of productions, the appearance of the architecture should be more timeless than timely and should avoid mannerisms that would identify the building as Ziegfeld, Brutalist, institutional, modern, or pop.

Other resources are provided for the audience in the trusses. The colors of the masonry infill panels at the exterior walls are warm

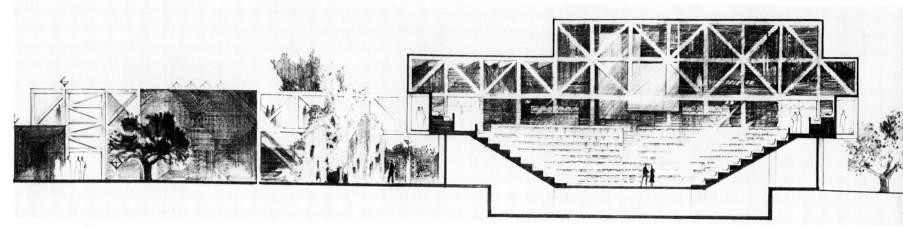

26.  Section of Greene's theater project, 1962

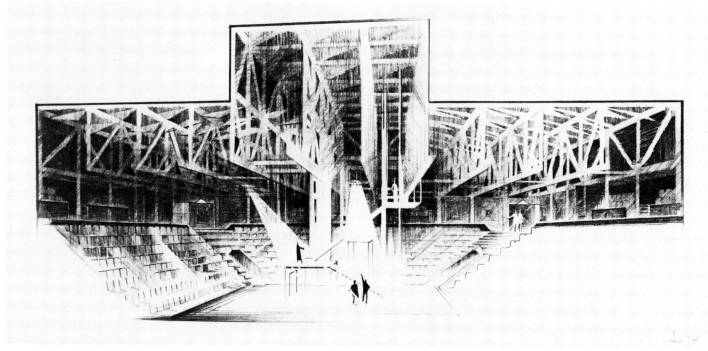

27.  Perspective of Greene's theater project

earth tones. The infilling of the truss is a very mild allusion to the half timber architecture of Elizabethan times, a period rich in dramatic associations. But most important is the deep space qualified by warm color. The Western tradition's appetite for the portentous suggestions of deep space is seen in the value it places on the paintings of Rembrandt, the vaulted Gothic cathedral, and the baroque style in general.

Rapoport and Kantor state a hypothesis about the way "ideals" evolve. (An "ideal" is defined as the maximum amount of stimulus complexity a person can assimilate at a given moment.) The experimenters introduce the term "pacer" and define it as a stimulus that has a "complexity value" a bit higher than the ideal in question. Pacers possess novelty, impact, unexpectedness, or ambiguity. Growth of an ideal takes place through a person's interaction with a pacer. Given his free choice, an individual will spend most of his time with the pacer stimuli. Most important, the experimenters have found that a common factor in pacer stimuli is an open-ended or indeterminate quality that can be called ambiguity, which requires that settled, known experience be bisociated with some model of indeterminateness.[2] Parted lips in the context of a dreamy expression on a human face provides both settled experience and the "whither, where" wonder of undetermined possibilities. Such an expression provides a perceptual model of known and ambiguous characteristics. Such a model can act as a means of both recovering and stabilizing a complexity ideal that is sought by the artist.

In section 5 it was argued that the artist projects elements of feeling into an image. An image that is successful in communicating a particular feeling gives the artist an opportunity to focus on that feeling and seek ways of heightening and extending its expression in subsequent works. The feeling expressed in the image embodies the current ideal and enables the artist to explore the type of feeling that may be considered the pacer, the more complex and profound feeling that is sought.

The Vermeer painting and Mayan head (figs. 10, 11) will serve as illustrations. The downcast eyes and parted lips of the classic Mayan head, less perfectly expressed, were present in Mayan sculptures for hundreds of years before the classical head was formed. Vermeer's early works show faces with the open lips and traces of the contemplative quietude and the ineffable sentience that he later developed so miraculously. The particular forms of earlier images, the early Mayan sculptures and the early Vermeers, may be seen as providing a complexity value for the artists that may have incited them to further development of that value in their images. Viewed in this light the image is not merely the record of human feeling, but an instrument for its development.

A particular feeling, here defined as an organized mass of reactions to experience, is difficult to summon up without the proper stimulus and even more difficult to verbalize. It extends into the layers of experience of which we may be only dimly aware if at all. Without a means of articulating types of feeling into some finite form, it is impossible for the artist to develop feelings to their maximum complexity and thus arouse deeper layers of experience. Once a type of complexity, for instance, the "open-ended sentience" referred to in the discussion of the Mayan head and the Vermeer, is objectified, both the artist and the beholder may become conscious of its elements.

# 9 IMAGES & MODELS

*The portrayal of an object by gesture rarely involves more than some one isolated quality or dimension, the large or small size of the thing, the hourglass shape of a woman, the sharpness or indefiniteness of an outline. By the very nature of the medium of gesture, the representation is highly abstract. What matters for our purpose is how common, how satisfying and useful this sort of visual description is, nevertheless.*

Rudolf Arnheim, *Visual Thinking*

The images of art give us a unique view of man's psychology and his insight. Very often as well as abstracting the phenomenal character of objects, they include perceptual models of the artist's conceptions of the physical and psychological world. The models need not resemble real experience or the visual world in appearance; rather, they allow us to get a focus on complex conceptions about the way the world works by illustrating some principle of construction or operation.

Models in art often play the same kind of role for artists as do the models in science for scientists. Scientific models do not match the exact physical processes or events they purport to represent; neither the "vortices" of Clerk Maxwell nor the "bent space" of Einstein are exact reproductions of physical realities. Yet such models are obviously of inestimable value for the development of thought. In an art image the principle of construction or operation demonstrated is not rendered in a measurable scientific sense, but in a sense that suggests an important phenomenal characteristic of its object. The hourglass shape of a woman, referred to by Arnheim as a gesture (one type of model), acts in this way. The shape is a visual feature we can use to organize much information that may be relevant to the intended meaning of the image. As one might infer from the example of the hourglass shape, the fact that an image contains a model has no necessary bearing on the quality of the image—an art image succeeds primarily as it elicits feeling. It may be argued, however, that certain art images are respected more for their role of providing models than for their ability to elicit feeling.

Many painters, consciously or otherwise, have sought means of expressing the connection of the events beyond an object represented in a painting to the object itself. In Picasso's remarkable painting of Dora Maar (fig. 28) the image of the head and body

28. Picasso's *Portrait de Dora Maar* (© *by S.P.A.D.E.M. Paris 1976*)

opens to merge with the field around it. This merging of figure and field acts as a model, suggesting to us that there is a meaningful background involving itself with the woman. Picasso's decisive opening of the figure into the field presents an economical visual organization to which a broad spectrum of experience can be attached. When expressed to the eye, as here, the model acts as "releaser" in the Gestalt sense. We recognize what we judge to be the meaning or intent of the model. This meaning then becomes a reference frame, often of major importance, for further evaluation of the image.

Another painting that dramatizes the linkage of a world in a background to events in a foreground is Rembrandt's *Jewish Bride*. The details of the glowing sleeve link it to an infinitely deep space, intimating a world of possibilities beyond the object. The sleeve is formed by an array of miraculously conceived golden shapes that appear to emerge from the intricacies of the deep space beyond the sleeve. The image presents us with a model, a conception of a finite object composed of an infinite number of entities housed in a background space, itself possessing infinite possibilities. The model becomes a reference to infinity to which particular experiences called up by the image can be attached—experiences, for instance, of warm colors, deep space, and man-woman relationships. The image-model also suggests that everyday objects are composed of underlying elements of matter, and it is in some ways analogous to the conception of matter and atomic entities that began as far back as the ancient Greeks and received scientific demonstration with Dalton.

Parallels between science and art are often found among the concepts with which men in these fields organize thought. It is as if scientists and artists draw upon a common stock of the ordering methods, generalizations, attitudes, and beliefs that prevail in a given era. It would seem natural that parallel expressions result. An example can be seen in the apparent relationship between the principles of Frank Lloyd Wright's architecture and those of contemporary science. The plan of the Martin house (fig. 24), like most of Wright's plans, is organized as a gradation of events radiating from an important node or terminal. The terminal acts both as climax and instigator of forces and tensions in the graded sequences. Wright tacitly presupposed this conception as an ultimate ordering principle; it infects all his designs, whether of carports or of colleges. The direct influence of Sullivan's treatment of ornament is likely, but on another level the conception was probably based on an analogy to growth patterns as explored in contemporary biology. It may also hold an unconscious reference to the notions of order that produced such turn-of-the-century conceptions as that of atomic structure, in which the heavy nucleus was visualized as a stable core in relation to its circling electrons.

It is interesting that certain models created in images have directly influenced the development of art, while others, perhaps expressive of deeper insights, have remained unused. Cezanne's structural conception of forms in space rendered on a flat canvas was influential as a model for certain artists that followed, such as Picasso. Vermeer, on the other hand, was able to construct an image of objects frozen in time in such a way that mind seems at one with matter. It is a more subjective concept, yet in Vermeer's best work it is pervasive. The consistency of his images makes one believe that they are informed by organizational and operational principles governing vision, objects, and mind; but the model is subtle and complex, and thus not readily grasped. It seems to have had no direct influence or parallel in painting, yet a similar concept was an unspoken presupposition of Newtonian science. One wonders about the influence Vermeer's paintings might have had if they had not dropped from sight for two hundred years. Perhaps his model was too subtle to be recognized, or perhaps it was the final expression of an unconscious world view that was not to be sustained.

For centuries men have tried to define the human mind and the thought process. Only within the last hundred years, however, have men deliberately tried to create models in literature that depict their conjectures of what mental processes are like. Such attempts to create images that present some concept of the mind in action have also occupied certain painters, as, for instance, Matta, who seems to achieve an image of activity inside the mind (fig. 29). For these artists new attitudes about the mind have acquired connections with attitudes about the scope of art. Earlier artists

63

64    29. Matta's *Le Vertige d'Eros* (*Museum of Modern Art, New York*)

had taken the mental process as an a priori condition, but for these innovators the extended understanding of art included data about mental processes that had not previously been expressed in art. The history of this change is an illustration of the evolution of a conception of art to include new content; at the same time it is a demonstration of the utility of the art image as a device to objectify new content through the use of models.

Possibly because of the influence of such artists as Matta, one of my intellectual aims in designing the Prairie House was to construct an image that could dramatize the cognitive process through which the mind determines the meaning of an object by drawing from a diversity of stored experience. The activity, the tensions, and the collected-together-at-an-instant aspects of the image are the outgrowth of this particular aim. I attempted a vivid expression of individually diverse experiences and an integration of these by the unification of the "different yet like" aspects of the experiences into a many-membered matrix. In this way I intended the image to develop a model demonstrating the cognitive process of the utilization of metaphor. Forms of creature, house, barn, and temple are organized within the design so that they can be recognized during a single act of perception.

Models in images can help us examine modes of ordering experience in the dynamically varying world of human interests. A classic example occurs in *Moby-Dick*, as Melville glides gracefully from chapters concerning the science and technology of whaling to chapters of metaphysical inquiry into the unconscious forces that motivate man. The two types of chapters imply a dialectic between the rational and the irrational. This mode of organization in *Moby-Dick* foreshadowed the conception of composition as the collection of relatively self-contained fragments, which Gertrude Stein developed as a meaningful form for the twentieth century. The fragments or separate songs in *Jesus Christ Superstar* may be seen not only as representing an attempt to organize the opera in response to the contemporary show business format of spot numbers, but also as reflecting the way the contemporary consciousness has come to make small unified packages out of the ever-increasing masses of information to which it is exposed. The television show *Mission Impossible* presents us with a sequence of visual packages: a man crawling through an air-conditioning duct, using high technology to accomplish his goal; a beautiful woman who speaks six languages seducing a prime minister; and so on. In this kind of presentation the story line is of little consequence; what counts is the excitement generated by the individual packages. The format allows the writers to fill each package with choice ingredients from the world of technology, foreign intrigue, sex, or whatever.

The placement of a collection of fragments within a field (which can be the edges of a painter's canvas or the thirty-minute time span of a television program) has become a prevalent model in contemporary art. The field is influenced by the character of the fragments contained within its limits and by the structural characteristics that may be designed into the field itself. For instance, in her play *Four Saints in Three Acts* Gertrude Stein presents what is in essence a collection of tableaux against a field, which, to use her words, becomes "a space of time filled with moving." The collection of characters—whether saints or pigeons—sometimes mills about, sometimes marches, sometimes is static. In the case of *Four Saints*, the field is without apparent design, although the design within the collections can be inferred to apply to the "space of time" in which they exist. In the paintings of Matta, the field is actually designed so that it seems to respond to the events within it. Events are shown with obvious three-dimensional relationships, but Matta's suggestion of several systems of events, spatially independent yet related, within the same picture produces an image strongly suggestive of a fourth dimension. This quality is perhaps heightened by his handling of the field at the location of certain events, as when the background space around the event is shaped or deformed in response to the event. The *Vertigo of Eros* provides a good example of this treatment.

Each of these illustrations presents a model that can assist us in three ways as we interpret the image in which it occurs. We can use the model to objectify organizational concepts within the image; we can use it as a tool to frame questions about our felt experience; and, finally, we can use it as a frame of reference to lift our enjoyment of the image to a level of higher complexity.

# 10 TEXTURE

*One sees the hardness and brittleness of glass, and when, with a tinkling sound, it breaks, this sound is conveyed by the visible glass. One sees . . . the hardness of a plane blade, the softness of shavings. The form of objects is not their geometrical shape. It stands in a certain relation to their specific nature and appeals to all our other senses as well. . . . Synaesthetic perception is the rule, and we are unaware of it only because scientific knowledge shifts the center of gravity of experience, so that we have unlearned how to see, hear, and, generally speaking, feel.*

Maurice Merleau-Ponty, *Phenomenology of Perception*

If any reader believes that texture is of minor importance in architecture, let him imagine what his feelings would be if the room in which he is now sitting were entirely lined with hair or, perhaps, stainless steel. Our responsive recognition of such contrasts makes it evident that texture is among the primary vehicles through which we understand the diversity of substances and materials in the world.

When we think of texture we often think of the graining or weave of an object's surface and the kind of tactile sensation it produces. Another important aspect of texture is its contribution to our awareness of the substance and structure of an object. When we speak of the "character" of a particular piece of stone, wood, or plastic, we are usually considering substance and structure. In forming our notion of the character of the object we use the data of graining, weave, or other dimensional interest of the surface, for many objects—such as stones and pieces of wood—through their textures give evidence of the nature of the substances that compose them and of the forces that produced them. Considered in this way, texture is a manifestation of the process by which an object is formed and not simply an arbitrary effect or a mere sense impression.

The traditions of classical Western architecture tend to ignore both the phenomenological and the symbolic values of textures. While the work of Le Corbusier and others has in some cases escaped the general rule, influences on the determination of form in the classical tradition have tended to be restricted to those of geometry and style. Consequently, the materials that have been used to fill in geometric and stylistic forms have been select-

ed without much regard for their aesthetic properties. This tradition has caused the opportunities for emotional effects produced by the colors and textures of materials to be minimized or lost entirely.

We instinctively respond to the color, degree of transparency, mass, and tactile characteristics of materials. Through this response we judge the tectonic or structural character of a building. Our stored experiences of stresses and strengths, along with our experiences of scale, provide criteria by which we unconsciously measure physical phenomena. It is here that the expressions of a master like Le Corbusier usually excel. For instance, the great mass and weight of the Marseilles Block (fig. 30), in an effect amplified by the texture and designed formwork patterns of the reinforced concrete, thrust down on the stout, tapering concrete piers in a dramatic statement of force acting through material, and one feels this through his own bodily experience. In many buildings executed in the manner of the Marseilles Block, such as the UNESCO building in Paris, the concrete piers seem no more substantial than cardboard. They give no sense of the forces being negotiated, nor does their texture give adequate indication of the intrinsic character of the material used to form them.

The neoclassic architects of the 1920s and the modernists of the Bauhaus devalued texture in much the same way. The Bauhaus architects, to be sure, emphasized the structural and functional character of new technological materials—the thin linear quality of

30. Le Corbusier's Unité d'Habitation in Marseilles, 1946-52 *(Ezra Stoller)*

steel members, for instance, and the transparency of large areas of glass—but in most of their architecture these materials and others were confined within the rectangular planes and boxlike volumes that were prescribed by the Bauhaus aesthetic. An imposed form dominating the material of which it is made prevailed in Bauhaus architecture and still prevails as a characteristic of much present-day architecture.

In the Shinto architectural tradition of old Japan, the expression of character through textures is an important concept. This tradition intuitively accepted the intercommunication of the senses which has been ignored by the Western tradition. In the Shinto tradition trees, stones, and other natural objects are revered for their characteristics of shape, texture, color, structure, and strength. Trees and stones, and their properties, are manifestations of a deified nature. They are to be cooperated with rather than conquered. It follows that the shapes of trees produced by natural forces, the textures and grain patterns of wood, and the changes in wood due to weathering are recognized and become part of the symbolic content of architecture.

In some of Frank Lloyd Wright's buildings, materials come to life in the spirit of the ancient Japanese, and at the same time express the possibilities of modern technology. The Johnson Wax Building (fig. 31), faulty in technique (it leaked) but magnificent in its image value, provides an illustration. Wright revealed the structural essences of materials which inform us vividly of the forces and

31. Frank Lloyd Wright's Johnson Wax Building, 1936 *(Reimar F. Frank)*

qualities found in nature. He also instinctively used the textural resources of materials for psychological effect. In his work the mass, transparency, color, and tactile qualities of materials are used in creative support of the purpose of the space enclosed. The materials and textures of a building for chemical research would be different from those of a bank, because human activities in these buildings are different and the building functions are different. In the Johnson Wax Building seemingly endless glass tubes of small diameter form translucent, irridescent bands where most buildings are confined by an opaque cornice. Light streaming unexpectedly from the junctures of wall, roof, and columns creates a surprising freedom and swimming translucency. The diffused light falls around the columns as it would fall around trees. In this building the glass tubes are perceived as being crystalline, watery, running continuously without end or beginning—making a perceptual model of the continuity that fascinated Wright. The whole effect is one of a poeticized, humanly scaled environment, formed from the most modern materials by the latest scientific methods and expressive of a physical principle of continuity. The technological innovations of the tubes, columns, and continuous walls seem to unite with the soft light, human scale, warm color, and shimmering glass. The image suggests a place where research is directed toward human ends.

The phenomenal and metaphorical properties of materials, to a large extent manifest in their textures, assist us in becoming aware of what we are like as organic beings. This is only natural, because we feel and know textures with bodies that have been produced by the same physical elements and forces that produce the textures we perceive. (The body is the primary agency through which we have learned our responses to the phenomenal world.) Knowledge of textures stems from experience that has been gained throughout life. As with exposure to other types of sensory stimulus, any experience of texture immediately evokes comparisons to similar experiences that have been linked within the mind to various knowledge-feeling responses.

The response to a stimulus is subject not only to the meanings adduced from stored phenomenal experience but also to the beliefs and dispositions of the beholder. Thus textureless, flat surfaces were valued by Bauhaus architects, who in planes and cubes saw industrial values, a purging of historical styles, and a verification of Euclidean truths. On the other hand, a contemporary conservationist sees redwood houses and leopard coats through filters that mar his enjoyment of the sensory detail of these objects. For while to most conservationists redwood and leopard skins are probably intrinsically more beautiful than synthetics, in a specific context sensory enjoyment must be coordinated with the extrinsic elements of use, purpose, and other personal and social considerations.

Much contemporary architecture takes no advantage of the emotional feelings and rich associations that are automatically awakened by textural cues. Warmth, coldness, hardness, and softness are among the coded experiences of life on earth and cannot be legislated out of the mind. Unless the user can take advantage of Bauhaus strategies for interpreting flat planes and cubes, a textureless architecture not only deprives him of an opportunity for relating to the external world, but forces him to deal with his previously coded experience of sterile surfaces.

Louis Sullivan, probably the most creative American architect of his era, demonstrated how textures can be among the details of architecture that give information about personal characteristics and life circumstances. This use of texture is clearly seen in two small tombs executed about 1890. The Getty tomb (fig. 32), for a woman who died young, is made of light grey limestone, carved in delicate reliefs like crystals, lace, snowflakes, and garlands. The designs glorify nature and life, but without causing the uneasy and contradictory feelings aroused by the textures and "realism" of the plastic flowers seen in cemeteries. Some of the designs are radial bursts, some are curling and entwined as if to represent some unending process. The cornice coping atop the tomb is scalloped in three uplifting rises. The overall textural effect has a delicate, lacelike aspect that can be associated with the feminine.

The Ryerson tomb was for a respected businessman and community leader, a long-time client of Adler and Sullivan. It is an unadorned pyramidal form of smooth, black granite. There is no carving other than a subtle, curving contour that spreads the base of

32. Louis Sullivan's Getty tomb, 1890

71

the tomb out and into the ground. Unusual stability and a masculinity that can be associated with the austere are communicated by the mass, shape, and texture.

Textural cues can also be structured into buildings for the living, where they can facilitate the issue of valued meanings and feelings established in the lived experience of particular users. Since the symbolic quality of a textural stimulus can be more important than the actual characteristics of surface, a designer must coordinate the sensory properties of materials with the meanings and associations that may be peculiar to the user's experience.

The house shown in figures 33-35, built in 1957, was designed for Catherine Lyne, a fifty-year-old lawyer. The level site, with many trees, is located in the suburbs of Houston, where the hot, humid climate does not lend itself to outdoor living. The plan of the house was conceived as a triangle with a triangular glassed-in light well enclosing a large beech tree at the center of the house. The floor was lifted to a height of three feet above the ground, allowing the site to be left largely as it was found. No lawn or border planting was necessary, and the single-story house gained height and an islandlike disposition.

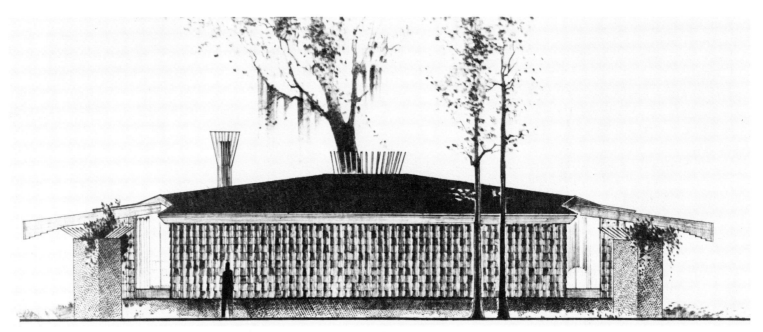

33. Elevation of Herb Greene's Lyne residence, 1957

The carport forms the place for arrival, with the carport roof sweeping visibly into the interior space of the house. Broad steps, planting, and storage elements screen the car from the interior space. One characteristic of the triangular plan is the tensive contrast between walls that open away from the viewer and walls that converge upon him. The interior space seems lively because of the contrast. Each corner of the triangle is cut off and filled with glass and a prismatic light well is centered in the triangle. The alignment of light well and windows allows either a vivid transparency giving one a view through the entire house or a noticeable sense of being walled in by large unbroken wall surfaces, as in a courtyard. The reflections on the facet-like glass walls of the light well help to enliven the interior, particularly at night.

The client, now deceased, had a law degree from the University of Texas. She had grown up in Beeville, Texas, and had moved to Houston to live near relatives. She was very tall with short, fairly straight, black hair and a raspy, masculine voice. A smoker of thin cigars she was bold of body and gesture and bolder of opinion ("the country should never have gone off the gold standard"). I was very much impressed with her clothes—one-of-a-kind corduroys and suedes. She enjoyed reminiscing about travel in Mexico, was interested in the preparation of Mexican food and in the culture of Mexico in general. She had some Mexican paintings and furniture and talked of acquiring more. We discussed materials and colors that she could live with.

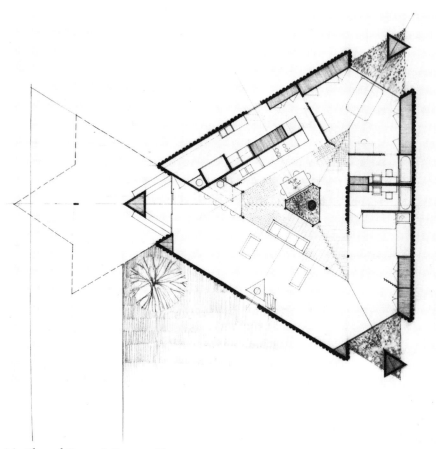

34. Plan of Greene's Lyne residence

73

35. Exterior of Lyne residence

Most architects and theorists disparage attempts to bridge the gap between user experience and the architect's interpretation of that experience, citing the lack of sufficiently precise tools of communication in the form of adequate questionnaires or other such objective checks on the collation of meanings. Facing an architect, many clients are reluctant to verbalize their feelings about housing. Americans, in particular, seem awed by experts; they sometimes lack verbal skills and in an era of increasing mobility and change are not sure what they can or should have in the way of a house. A human being can live in almost anything and often chooses his dwelling to conform to social symbol systems which have little or nothing to do with his inner character, needs, and aspirations. Moreover, we have few precedents and value systems that encourage a dialogue aimed at getting to the existential first principles relating a user to his house.[1] Even if the user can communicate his experience, art is required to reconstitute that experience into architecture. It is not surprising that architects seek more manageable tasks, and it is obvious that in this period of inflationary costs, social change, and environmental crisis other matters seem more pressing. But for a creative, human architecture the response to user character and consciousness remains as an aesthetic and philosophical necessity.

For my part, remembering Louis Sullivan's statement that sympathy is the most important of the architect's powers, I approach the task with an attempt to develop conversations with clients in order to encourage them to communicate their experiences and attitudes. Some of the results of this approach can be seen in sections 18 and 19. Suffice it to say here that many of the client's recurring dispositions for forms, colors, and textures can be identified from his verbal descriptions of his experience and attitudes and from his physical gestures and personal possessions. If the architect can establish these dispositions of the client in association with appropriate cues of human scale, shelter, and other basic ingredients of architecture, then an environmental matrix that allows the client to communicate with his experiential resources can result.

Catherine Lyne conveyed to me that she liked to be surrounded with natural materials, wood in particular. She objected to the ticky-tack subdivision housing sprouting all over Houston. She didn't like to look at flat-roofed houses nor to be squashed by flat ceilings. She had gas wells back in Beeville but was wary of spending a great deal of money and wary also of architects' legendary failures to meet budgets. She set a $35,000 limit—enough in 1957 to build a substantial small house.

The walls and sloping ceilings of the house were framed with the wood studs and rafters familiar to the house-building trades. The interior walls and ceilings were finished in one-by-four-inch beveled fir boards of vertical grain. Exposed beams and columns, also fir, were formed into a precise geometric arrangement integrated with the triangular interior plan. All the wood was stained a low-luster

medium honey color. The overall texture was of pronounced but controlled linear patterns that massed together to avoid an abrasively busy appearance.

The exterior surface of the walls was covered with barrel-shaped clay roofing tiles of dark red, purple, and brown, hung in vertical rows with about an inch of weathered copper showing between the tiles. The effect was one of mass and substance with the shelter cues usually found in a roof prominently reconstituted in the unbroken walls. The tiles, of course, can be seen in a Mexican context. They also recall, remotely, the scales of creatures. A rich texture with vaguely primordial secondary illusions is produced. Gaudí had used the lapped roofing tiles for their associations with an animate world. Bruce Goff and several of his students at Oklahoma were also interested in this effect. The shingles and boards of the Prairie House (frontispiece, figs. 13, 14) are even more easily associated with creatures because of more pronounced creature gestalts in the outlines of the house.

Gertrude Stein wrote about people becoming like their given names, playfully asserting that these parallels must not be pressed. Yet it is interesting to think of the similarities among all the people named Frank that one has known. Bruce Goff believed that people developed affinities with their last names, also. He once did a house project for a client named Swombat. This house, set in the Indiana dunes, had a long swooping covered passage from house to car, rather like a tail. Crusty Catherine Lyne's house got forceful, geometric lines and earth tiles on its walls.

The design intentions for color are similar to those for textures. The honey-colored stain of the interior walls—transparent in order to reveal the wood grain—attempts to involve the user in a color that seems to emanate from within the material rather than to lie on the surface as flat paint seems to do. Merleau-Ponty speaks of the essence behind color, "a somber power which radiates from the object, even when it is overlaid with reflective light." The effect produced by the mass of our experience and activated by our perception of the colored object he sees as an immediate and persistent presence in the object.[2] It is such a persistent quality, with positive associations for the user, that the designer seeks to establish. The design process requires the accommodation of learned experience of color to its historical meanings and contexts; likewise it requires the use of such bits of general psychological knowledge as the fact that violet is enervating while red is dynamogenous. Finally the designer must remain flexible enough to decide which colors best serve a particular design situation that must take into account a changing present.

In the case of the honey-colored stain in Catherine Lyne's house, the shade was selected because of its cheerfulness and its harmony with the clay tiles and some of the user's clothing, and because of the user's preference for full-bodied hues rather than pastels.

In the approach to architecture advocated in this work, texture is not regarded as an arbitrary decoration. Nor is it regarded merely as an expression of the functional enclosure of the walls of a building. Texture becomes a quality of a surface that mediates between the user and the building on the one hand, and between these two and the rest of the world on the other. Texture should be developed in such a way that it will communicate most clearly the character of the particular user-building situation. The designer determines the character of the user-building situation by using in combination form archetypes associated with the particular building types[3] and forms derived from existential aspects of the situation such as the personality of the user. The climate and site are also taken into consideration.

The process of combination calls for an imaginative readiness to appropriate, modify, or discard gestalts relating to the user within the repertory of building forms and materials. In selecting a building form that would correspond to some of my notions of Catherine Lyne, for example, I wanted an image that could be read as a house for one person. An equilateral triangle or a circle can be read as a form that possesses singleness and compactness. For Miss Lyne, the triangle was selected because it also possessed dynamism and angularity—qualities that I felt were more suited to her physiognomy and personality.

Actually, to abstract relevant features from the physiognomy, personality, intentions, and outlooks of people and to incorporate such features in images is as old as portraiture. However, architecture does not permit the

76

36. Elevation of Greene's school project, 1951

physiognomic congruence that we see between Houdon's sculpture of George Washington, for example, and the Washington of real life. The use of physiognomic characteristics in architecture is confined to more abstract levels. Considering the low state of the art I suppose we should be thankful. Another difference between architecture's portraiture and Houdon's lies in the fact that a sum-up statement seems to be expressed in Houdon's sculpture of Washington, while none is attempted in architecture. According to Sir Kenneth Clark, Houdon created Washington in the image of a "Roman Republican hero, a decent country gentleman, called away from his farm to defend his neighbors' liberties."[4] The image of her house does not represent

any comparable summary of Catherine Lyne. The image is admittedly only one possibility of many, in which forms, textures, and colors corresponding to selected aspects of Catherine Lyne's personality and experience might have been provided for her enjoyment.

The drawings in figures 36-38 are of an unexecuted project that expresses ideas about form and order in architecture as heightened by texture and also ideas about human behavior and needs. Although the project dates from my student days and leaves unsolved many problems of program, building topology, and construction technique, it incorporates certain ideas that continue to interest me.

77

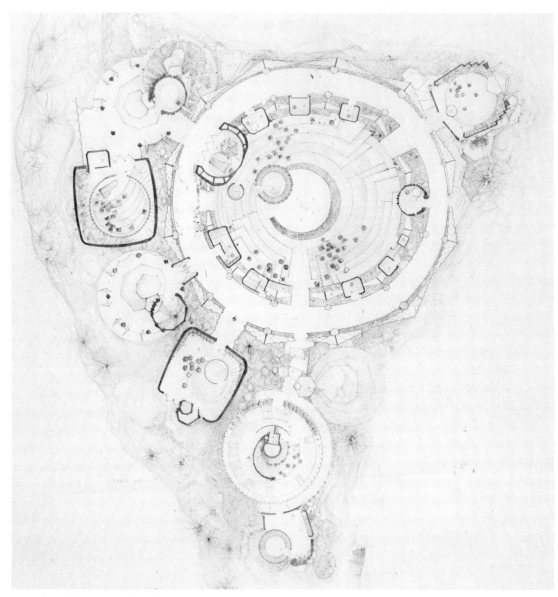

37.  Plan of Greene's school project

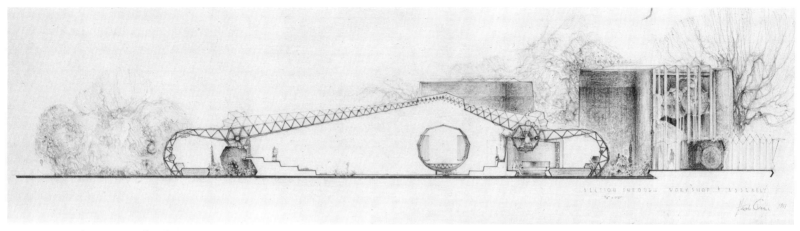

38. Section of Greene's school project

The program called for an arts complex for high school students in a private school. The site was in the environs of Oklahoma City where the prairie met a rather wild wooded area with a pond and a stream. Since the building was to be used as a place of learning for people in an impressionable and formative period of their lives, it was conceived as a presentation of a variety of forms and spaces that could allude to accumulated experience of nature, the self, and social relations. A primary aim was to provide an imaginative demonstration of how building materials could foster an understanding of the textures and forms that are found in nature.

Human affinities with nature remind us that the human organism has evolved out of the same elements that compose the rest of the natural world. Manifestations of natural forces are identified with unchangeable needs of human life and ignite primeval emotions because man perceives himself to be of the earth. With these ideas in mind, I chose the materials to be used in the school for their associations with such natural structures as earth, water, and stones. The materials would dramatize contrasts of the bright and the dull, the smooth and the rough, the hard and the soft, and the opaque and the translucent. Such contrasts affect our feelings and facilitate our orientation in a phenomenal world.

Spaces for specialized and in some cases noisy activities, such as music, crafts, painting, and sculpture, were provided in separate, thick-walled concrete structures whose integral exposed aggregates merged with applied earth-colored terra-cotta blocks and beads. The students could make and apply some of the pottery and beads themselves. These spaces, textured like simpler Carlsbads, each had one large glass wall that folded onto the roof plane as a skylight to provide ample studio light and also to furnish a signal or cue that they were used as studios. The transparency of the wall and roof would break open the heavy, enveloping mass in an unexpected manner, giving an effect rather like the broken forms of some geodes or the protective shells of seed pods. The forms were chamfered and softened to offer analogies to the shapes of living organisms.

Within the concrete structures were individual workspaces, practice rooms, storage modules, and other individualized enclosures that were suspended or otherwise supported in a functional arrangement of usable space. The textures of these interior spaces, the forms of which were rather like capsules or pods, were those of fabrics or soft materials that need not protect against the weather but could contribute visual and acoustical values. The image of a large space sheltering several smaller spaces sets up references to nature in the areas both of biological growth and of family hierarchy. The perceptual form suggests seed pods, protective shells, the cellular worlds seen in a microscope, and perhaps even planets orbiting a sun.

Contrasting with the massive, thick walls and the Carlsbad-like textures of the studio buildings were diaphanous glass and metal structures, which were like harbors where people might come together. Used for seminar rooms, galleries, and lounges, they were places where students could gather, located between the music, art, and drama studios. An important characteristic of the surface of these spaces solved problems arising out of their orientation to the path of the sun. Opaque and translucent colored insulating glass panels were graduated to clear glass panels in order to block out the hottest rays of the sun while admitting light and view to the north and east. The overall effect would be that of dome-shaped forms faceted and banded with a graded sequence of colors responding to the azimuth of the sun.

An influence on this project which should be mentioned parenthetically is the work of Frank Lloyd Wright. Wright's interest in plants and sea shells as models for architecture, his use of dramatically contrasting materials, and, most important, his use of visual terminals are reflected in this design. Wright's terminals, more fully described in the discussion of models and images, tend to be fixed centers that act as focal points for the outlying elements of his design.

In the school project, however, I attempted to allow the user more latitude in composing his own visual terminals than he would have in a Wright building. My purpose was to create the illusion that the terminals had fluid or shifting centers. One design device supporting this aim was a plan that did not rely on parallel lines. Each major enclosure could be perceived "in-the-round," which is to say that more than one of its sides, as well as parts of the top and bottom, would be visible from any given vantage point. Several enclosures could be seen at one time because of the complex distribution of glass. Small changes in the position of the viewer would reveal varied dispositions of contrasting forms, with the result that overlapping forms would tend to be massed into visual terminals that would vary with the point of view of the user. It was hoped that an environment of varied but harmonized forms and textures, arranged according to hierarchies of use and size, sequences of textures, and other ordering devices, would create a spatial experience increasing and enhancing the viewer's awareness of his location as he moved through the complex. A vivid sense of orientation would be achieved by the provision of perceptual cues in more than one mode. That is why varied texture, color, and lighting and the perception of forms in three dimensions are important to this design.

Although the forms are ordered, the spatial organization appears to be fluid; the viewer would have to recover order from an organization that is apparently random. This characteristic supports the aim of creating a shifting terminal of interest. Actually the whole complex is related to a dominant circulation path that can be readily grasped. This is the perimeter passage around the largest multiuse space.

The variations in texture, color, and lighting would offer, in addition to perceptual contrasts, contrasting environments for varied activities. Spaces for isolated work and individual contemplation are connected by pathways to the major spaces. Smaller and larger spaces occur as if by chance. Some spaces are hard to find and some are hard to get to. The largest meeting place would accommodate the entire department of students, but it is ar-

ranged as a set of terraces with ceilings scaled so that small groups could also be comfortable. The disposition of all the forms is calculated not to reflect abstract conceptions of order based on symmetry and Euclidean forms, but to suggest an array of natural spaces that are somehow useful and scaled to man.

It is an important and sometimes a formidable task for image makers to create a relevant background for the primary objects and figures that are presented in an image, as a painter must do when he presents a figure against a ground. Rembrandt excelled in creating a feeling of heightened interaction between figures and their grounds. He developed a unique way of presenting figures emerging from a space usually rendered as warm, infinitely deep, and richly suggestive of potential meanings that seemed to inform his foreground figures. A general condition of the ground is that its details must be sufficiently vague to allow the viewer a breadth of interpretation. At the same time, the details of the ground must be explicitly related to the object in the foreground so that analogies, suspended judgments, and possible links between background and object are possible.

The interiors of the Lyne and Joyce (see fig. 58) residences are conceived in a manner that is, in a sense, similar to the figure-ground method of composition. The textures, colors, and structural details of the walls are backgrounds designed to relate to particular experiences and characteristics of users. The user, in this context, becomes the foreground figure.

Recent technologies have produced materials and techniques that may be used to create specific environmental backgrounds. Polyurethane foam seems particularly well adapted to create both textures and forms that can respond to the individuality of user experience. It is to be hoped that a way will soon be found to reduce the extreme flammability of this material. Used now primarily as thermal insulation, the foam can be sprayed onto armatures or into molds. It has the ability to produce a number of different textures as the consistency of the mixture and the pressure of the spray applicator are varied. It also conforms with great accuracy of detail to whatever mold it is sprayed or poured against. The material can cover with a precise cocoon almost any object rich in association for a user. Such an object as, for instance, an old Buick radiator, could be incorporated into the walls of one's house. While any objects and shards associated with a user's experience could be incorporated into the forms and textures of his domain, the success of such a venture is subject to the constraints of concept and execution that accompany any art form; otherwise the result might be no more effective than baby shoes preserved in plastic. But with the suggestions offered by the arranged collections of a sculptor such as Nevelson, an image background pertinent to a user's lived experience seems possible.

The use of urethane foam, as of any material, raises questions about matching sensory stimulation with meanings that are appropriate to the context of the stimulus. Whether the plastic foam is biodegradeable and whether foam textures can be designed to overcome their uncomfortable affinities with intestinal lining would be questions for some users. My view is that coatings and textured surfaces can overcome the slippery quality of the foam and the distaste we have for the chemically derived product.

A changing environment produces changes in strategies for interpreting materials. Bricks have been and continue to be one of man's favorite building materials. Bricks are of the earth. We can feel the control we have over a building unit that has been scaled to our own hands. Current economic and technological conditions, however, discourage the use of brick in architecture. The handcraft piece-by-piece methods of construction that date back to antiquity seem obsolete and inappropriate. The school project illustrated in figures 36-38 was an attempt to make a model for coordinating current technology with the need to maintain ageless ties with earthy materials. The students would cast pottery blocks and beads of their own design and apply them to certain parts of the building. This kind of exercise becomes a participatory experience in art and craft. The earthy textures of the applied ceramics would contrast with the watery transparencies made possible by latest technologies of plastics, glass, and metals.

The participation of the users in the building process was an important intention. The rise of the modern industrial state has tended to cut society off from a knowledge of the construction of the buildings in which it works and lives. Nowadays specialists construct our buildings; the rest of us who use them know little of how they were put together and seem to care less. We are accumulating evidence that man needs both physical and conceptual involvement to establish deeper relationships with his environment. An important contribution of technology would be the provision of the means for more people to enter into the process of constructing their personal environment.

Some architects are attempting to devise strategies that allow the user more opportunities for shaping his house. The Archigram of England is a group of designers who advocate inflatable, mobile, and short-lived structures for housing as alternatives to the expensive traditional buildings currently available. The short-lived structures are conceived as components that can be purchased separately, assembled, demounted, and reassembled. I am by no means critical of the social, economic, and technological reforms advocated by the Archigram, but many of its proposals clearly reflect a devaluation of the intrinsic sensory properties of materials. The group recommends extensive use of vinyl and metal containers for human occupancy without research into how the surfaces of such containers will wear on human sensibilities. The fascination with mobility, camping, life-support hardware, disposable enclosures, technology, and a new social organization seems to have obscured the question of what effects a lifetime spent in renewable plastic tents and capsules can have on a man. I would deplore the sweeping acceptance of any intellectual strategy that does violence to our accumulated experiences of the textures of a natural world.

83

# 11 SITE RELATIONSHIP

*At dawn the buttes of the Grand Canyon lie sunk in darkness below the continental rim. Slowly the red light models their sides, revealing their bastions step by step, the vastest and most strictly constructed architectural forms on the continent and still, after all their aeons, wholly ignorant of man. No human dialogue can engage their archaic presences: a Greek temple would be riding chaos on their mesas, a Gothic cathedral lost among the spires. Far to the south, indeed, the temple bases of Mexico echo their forms and in a more manageably sacred landscape, call the mountains to themselves; but there are no such temples here.*

Vincent Scully, *American Architecture and Urbanism*

Bertalanffy defines an organism as a hierarchy of parts and processes, interwoven and overlapping so that the organism constantly gives to and receives from the outside world.[1] From that definition can be derived a model that many architects, most notably Frank Lloyd Wright, have used as a guide. In this section it will be shown how some features of the organic model may be expressed in the relationship of architecture to the site.

The human need to relate architecture to site stems ultimately from the ecological relationships of the climate, soils, plants, and animals of the earth's regions. Survival and evolution depend upon cooperation. For a creature with the mobility and consciousness of man, cooperation takes two forms—the physical and the symbolic. Physical cooperation is essential for man's survival; conservation of resources of all kinds has become an

obvious necessity. A consideration of the psychological or symbolic characteristics of site relationship is also important, because we recover consciousness of our biological being when we become aware of the symbolic cooperation between the man-made and the natural environment. Symbols of this cooperation are considered here to be among the most valued archetypes for inclusion in images.

Another aspect of site relationship is the symbolic link certain objects and ideas have with particular places and regions. The ancient artifacts of a place, like the legends attached to it, can constitute valued evidence of the lives of previous inhabitants. Such evidence can also be found in the folk buildings or other architectural forms that may have resulted from physical cooperation with a site. It can be found in landforms, rivers, and

39. Frank Lloyd Wright's Millard house, 1920 *(Wayne Andrews)*

other natural features that have become associated with historical events. Buildings and natural features acting as signs of valued past experience permit a communion—vague, perhaps, but beneficent—that can help bind together a social group and enable people to feel that they are part of a historical process larger than their immediate lives.

In the Millard house (fig. 39) we see an architecture that is a symbolic response both to the physical character of a site and to the architecture of earlier inhabitants of the region. The relationships of the textures, patterns, and geometric masses of this house to the physical site will be discussed in section 15. The issue of the relationship of the Millard house to architecture of an earlier aboriginal civilization warrants discussion here. One may wonder why Wright chose references to Indian cultures rather than to the culture of Spanish colonials or other early inhabitants. Wright admired the fit to the land that the pueblos and ornamented stone cities of pre-Columbian architecture possessed, a fit that was, for the most part, lacking in the architecture of the European Renaissance. The influences of the Japanese, English Tudor, and modern European architecture were also absorbed into Wright's creations, but the Mayan and Miztec influences in the block house of Southern California remain unmistakable.

California has a scale and vegetation (and also an atmosphere, before the advent of six million automobiles) that make an enchanted landscape, probably unmatched in its beauty in any other American state. This enchantment stimulated the romantic tendency of the imagination to bring the far near and to prefer a softness and lyricism of expression to the strict, reductionism characteristic of a Mondrian. The Millard house, romantic in its appropriation of Mayan form and in its softness of texture, was built in 1920, ushering in a period that lasted until about 1930 and saw Picasso produce lyrical drawings of archaic females and Stein write a novel described as a romantic landscape. Much even of the eclectic architecture of the day was soft and blurry, like Bertram Goodhue's works in the Spanish style. A romantic tendency was in the air.

Wright had built a warehouse with a pronouncedly pre-Columbian frieze in Wisconsin in 1917. It is a fine piece but somewhat disturbing to me. The Mayan allusion seems out of place in Wisconsin, especially in a warehouse. The use of a historical reference in architecture requires a delicate balance among the physical characteristics of a site, the level of familiarity of the reference to the user, and the connotations of the use of the building. The balance requires attention to the organic fit of the appropriate reference to the new situation. The Millard house is more successful than the Wisconsin warehouse in this respect.

In many cases past experience has become interwoven with the physical features of the land as altered in ecologically undesirable ways or as linked to some unfounded bit of legend. The moors of England were once covered with forests, and only gradually in the course of history became the open, wild heath that inspired English writers of the nineteenth century. But to reforest the heath and restore the ancient ecological balance would disrupt the ecology of human associations and history which have become a part of the English literary tradition and consequently the cultural memory of all English-speaking peoples.[2] Similarly, the American prairies are connected in people's minds with the heroic figure of the cowboy created by the dime novel and the movies—a fabricated image with little relation to reality. But the prairies, like the moors, can inspire anthems of national experience in spite of ecological and historical inconsistencies. Such landscapes remain resources for the imagination in the creation of new man-made environments to be set in their midst.

To make proper use of these resources requires a creative integration on a much higher level than the building of an imitation Gothic abbey or of a "frontier city" amusement park. The psychological resources of the physical forms and of the legends of landscapes should be used in environmental design as part of a firm intellectual aim to interweave man's present experience with his past. I think this is ultimately no less important to human well-being than the shaping of environment in response to utilitarian function, behaviorist principle, or abstract aesthetic.

If architects are not interested, Disneyland developers are. The popular interest in "frontier cities" and other such nostalgic endeavors attest a human need. The commercial interests responsible are so careful and patronizing

40. John Lautner's Elrod house, 1968 *(Leland Y. Lee)*

of their audience that they stifle any chance for authentic art, but the success of the developments should be an indication of the potential value of allusion to the past, whether legendary or historical. It seems a perversion that the creation of large-scale environments that seriously incorporate semblances and reminders of human life of earlier times should be left to the devisers of amusement parks.

A desert ridge in Palm Springs, California, is the site of the house illustrated in figure 40. It is recessed into the ridge, and from the approach drive the largest part of the roof is seen as a continuation of the desert itself, planted with yellow flowers. At a time when man's houses are sprawling out to obscure the land he so highly prizes, this garden makes a meaningful gesture. But it is the interior of the main living space that shows the power of an architect to seize the visual essence of a site and reconstitute it into an image. The brittle textures, tawny color, and angular forms of the desert are both boldly and subtly counterpointed by the designed forms of concrete roof and mitered glass. Wedge-shaped openings in the roof provide light and shade in response to the earth's movement around the sun. The architect, John Lautner, achieved an almost primal sense of shelter by recessing the house into the desert and by carefully expressing the thickness and mass and, consequently, the weight of the concrete.

In spite of the great sense of mass and

weight, the space as a whole is uncommonly free. The roof, a tentlike sixty-foot circle, produces a visual freedom that seems impossible. The total impression is one of a unique synthesis of technological skill, exhilarating freedom, closeness to the earth, shelter, and a glamour that is appropriate to the life-style of the owner—a nationally known interior designer—and to the climate of Southern California.

Most of us are fearful of the expense suggested by the labor of fitting glass to irregular boulders and of forming the concrete tent. Our system of free enterprise produces many individual houses just as costly but few that can match this one in symbolizing our organic connection with the forces and forms of nature.

In sharp contrast to the desert site of the Elrod house is the location in rolling hills of the Kentucky Bluegrass of the house shown in figures 41-43. The house is large enough so that in both plan and elevation it rolls with the surrounding hills. This is a result of the architect's conceiving the house as a "street" one hundred sixty-five feet long which all members of a family of six must traverse in their daily round of activities. There is no "east wing" to get lost in. The land is welcomed into the house by walls that extend out to form terraces and courts.

Kentucky has deep green foliage and not very many cloudless days. White stucco is handsome and usually without glare in this environment. It relates well to the white

41. Exterior of Greene's Lovaas house, 1968 *(Bill Strode)*

fences and antebellum houses and to the many vernacular buildings in the Bluegrass area, as well as to the user's avowed interest in Spanish architecture. The roof is low and spreading, with an overhang of five feet along the length of the house. It is protective and its suggestion of ranch house architecture is appropriate to the users, though not to Kentucky. To make the house seem at home in Kentucky the end walls are formed without an overhang—a prominent characteristic of many houses in the Bluegrass. It also is a device that produces a reminiscence of Spanish architecture. The best view is toward the north and the house is oriented in this direction. So that sunlight can penetrate the interior, a clerestory formed by the juncture of the roof planes traverses the entire length of the house on the southern exposure.

42. Interior of Greene's Lovaas house *(Bill Strode)*

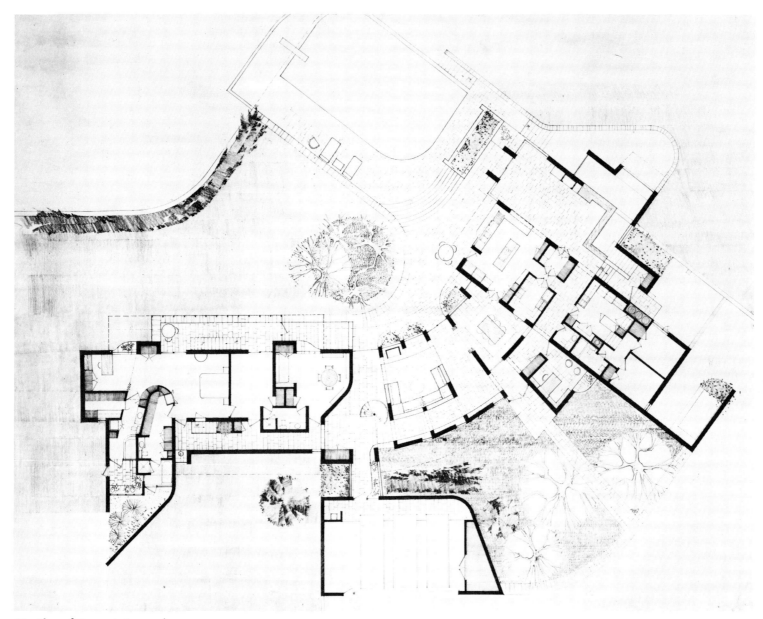

43. Plan of Greene's Lovaas house

44. Greene's Unitarian church, 1965 *(Bob Bowlby)*

An architectural response to a site can begin with a symbolic gesture that is expressive of an attitude of the users toward the site. The modest Unitarian church in figure 44 is centered on a seven-acre suburban site that is treated as a small park. The low windows of the meeting space lean out to focus attention on the land and the earthly world. This congregation is oriented more toward the world than toward heaven. Funds budgeted for tree planting on the perimeter of the site are usually diverted to social causes. Thus the symbolic gesture of the windows connects the seated congregation with the land and community. To dramatize the idea that the windows are continuous and that the interior space is enveloping and yet free, the roof is expressed as a sheltering umbrella.

While some determinants of site relationship are symbolic, many are produced by direct physical cooperation with a site. In the Prairie House (frontispiece, figs. 13, 14) there are a number of physical determinants. The severe windstorms of Oklahoma almost always approach from a direction just south of west. The narrow end of the house points due west so that the house presents a small, well-braced target from that direction. The sun, a particularly beautiful image as it rises and sets in this part of the country, is accepted by the kitchen and the family room at the east end and at the west end by the living room. During the heat of the day the sun is screened out by walls.

The first level of the house is about four feet above grade. It is connected to the ground by a ramp spreading out to the entrance drive. Thus the house is treated like a peninsula in a sea of prairie, and the need for landscaping around the base of the house is avoided. Board and shingle textures are at home in the windswept, natural condition of the site and also are in keeping with the weathered wood of the farm buildings that dot the region.

# 12 VERNACULAR

*The folk tradition is much more closely related to the culture of the majority and life as it is really lived than is the grand design tradition.*

Amos Rapoport, *House, Form, and Culture*

A discussion of architectural images would be incomplete without a consideration of vernacular architecture—the folk building of pre-industrial times. Generally, vernacular buildings provide messages that human hands and heads are in control of an environment. The handcrafted materials used, human scale, spaces derived from social needs, and forms responding to the exigencies of climate all help to convey these messages. In addition vernacular buildings offer the surprise and relief of the "unplanned," harmonized by similarities of materials, forms, and technologies. This combination of chance with the order derived from a limited range of materials and forms usually brings a pleasing degree of visual complexity and ambiguity of the kind we observe in the European hill town or the Japanese farm village. The processes of vernacular building also provided a context in which the user participated in acts of construction within fairly static cultural and technological boundaries that contributed to an orderly growth.

The social and technological situations that produced vernacular buildings have practically vanished. Whether we can employ the vernacular for much more than a source of visual cues is a difficult question. The visual aspect must not be undervalued, however. In the hands of Le Corbusier the visual cues of vernacular architecture inform a Ronchamp. The thick whitewashed forms, the small openings, and the rough textures of Ronchamp, often considered among the purest of contemporary architecture's creations, are in the tradition of the vernacular building of the Mediterranean. Yet Le Corbusier seems to have denied any influence from vernacular building. Like most of the architectural progressives of his day he addressed social and technological reforms. Ronchamp, however, is rich in metaphor from a much broader area. Le Corbusier's remarks about his famous design stress the solutions to problems of lighting and acoustics encountered in designing for the celebration of the Mass but do not touch upon the thick, white-washed walls and towers that so strikingly resemble earlier Mediterranean architecture.

The rational modern mind is hard put to defend the use of forms derived from a past that is believed to be technologically and so-

93

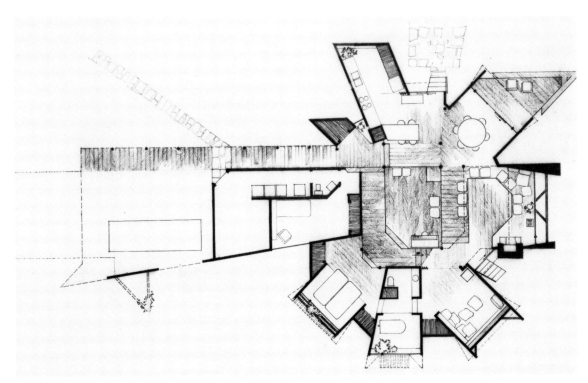

45. Plan of Greene's DeLuca residence project, 1973

cially obsolete. The obvious attachment of so many people to images derived from the vernacular has been dismissed by rationalists as a condition in which sentimentality is mixed with ignorance. But such images can be carriers of psychological values independent of the buildings in which they were originally established. Images from the vernacular of the early Kentucky farmhouse appear in plans of a contemporary house for the Bluegrass (figs. 45, 46). Near the rural site of the house stands the stone and timber ruin of a pioneer farmhouse. One prominent characteristic of

the early farmhouse is the addition of shed-like appendages to the main house to meet changing needs. The human activities linked to these additions are those of clearing the land, securing the family as it expanded, and establishing the community.

The users of the house would be interested in pioneer building no matter where they lived, since they, like pioneers, consider themselves to be making a fresh start. Interested in organic gardening and in developing the natural features of their farm, they seek a lifestyle that reflects an awareness of nature and

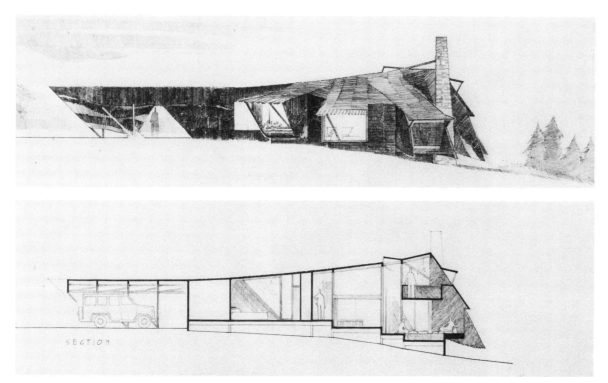

46. Section and elevation of DeLuca residence project

an understanding of ecology. The users are not much attracted by the polite vernacular of the Bluegrass. They have not lived in the area long enough to develop an attachment to its white-columned mansions with manicured lawns, nor would they be in sympathy with the society and the state of mind that produced these houses. Thus the users seem to have a more positive imaginative link with pioneer families and houses than with aristocratic landowners and their antebellum mansions.

An image can be composed of many ele-

ments; the add-on, shedlike appendage was absorbed into the visual form of the new house. That many vernacular buildings with such appendages are poor in aesthetic value is not sufficient reason to dismiss the importance of their symbolic value. Vernacular buildings are messages from the past, relating details of the human settlement of a region. By the incorporation of visual reminders of the earlier settlements in the new, a resource is made available for the users and the beholders to keep them in closer touch with human history.

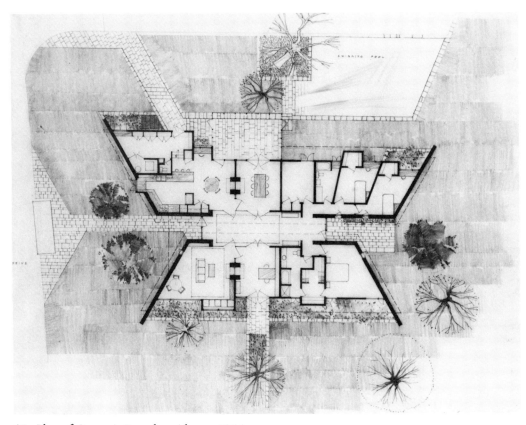

47. Plan of Greene's French residence, 1966

Possibly the most viable sources of connection between the vernacular and the new are the social and climatic determinants that are often inseparable from the visual forms of the vernacular. The high-ceilinged central hall in early houses in Kentucky, for instance, acted as entrance, organizer of interior space, and air conditioner as well. A contemporary response to the early hall of the vernacular can be seen in figures 47-49. This residence stands near Shaker buildings and other early post-pioneer Kentucky houses admired by the users, who have lived all their lives among these buildings. More important, the users express a good deal of sympathy for the pastoral social life of Kentucky, the origins of which go back to the simple brick houses with porches and tall windows that made the humid summer climate more tolerable. The ceiling heights in the old buildings range from ten to fourteen feet. The walls are thick, usually a foot or more of masonry, with plastered surfaces. Built-in cabinets and simple wood trim were among the many characteristic details admired by the clients. The architect was charged with providing an imaginative reconstruction of certain of these features in a plan that had strict economic limitations as well as strict functional requirements peculiar to the program of the owners.

The organizational preferences of the owners were these: unusually small, defined rooms (characteristic of some of the early houses); a central hall; and maximum contact with the farmland outside. The resolution of the hall proportions was of major importance in the design. The hall is thirteen feet six inches high, a reflection of the high-ceilinged old buildings. Its length is primarily a result of the dimensions and layout of the other rooms with some adjustment made by the walls of the end rooms on each side, which splay out to form entrances to the hall. The width was chosen to produce proportions that evoke the feeling of the older houses and to satisfy the apparent functional and aesthetic requirements for this particular hall. The room is well bathed in natural light; the ends are fully glazed, and a skylight, like the horse barn monitors of the region, runs full length. Although the visual extension of the ends of the hall through glass walls promotes a feeling of freedom, the feeling of the room as a whole is that of a contained space. The space is formed by a disposition of cues recalling the users' favored type of Kentucky architecture. Symmetrically opposed series of French doors with bands of glass above admit light from the forty-foot length of skylight to most of the rooms of the house and extend visual contact with the skylight into the rooms. Certain walls are detailed to reveal a thickness of a foot or more.

Human scale is introduced by the French doors and the low eave line (six feet six inches), which is visible from all parts of the hall when the many doors are open. The hall is remarkable for the open-ended character of the feeling it produces. There are two principal reasons for this: visual contact with the trees and farm beyond is maintained in every part of the hall; and the disclosure of the

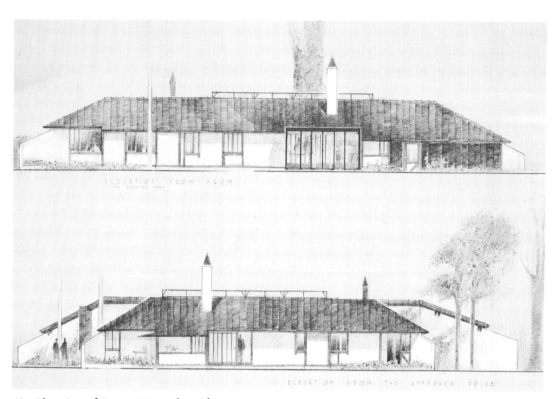

48. Elevation of Greene's French residence

97

49. Interior of Greene's French residence *(Bill Strode)*

entire form of the house by the organization of the room produces a visual complexity and a sense of indeterminant possibilities, the underlying order notwithstanding. Important psychic messages are provided by the ambiguity of containment in small, definite rooms with simultaneous awareness of spaces beyond, and also by the juxtaposition of the low scale of six feet six inches with the high Kentucky scale of thirteen feet six inches. The white walls, the honey-colored wide boards of the floors, and the painted trim are strong local allusions. A literal translation of Kentucky vernacular is avoided, although the space includes psychological touchstones derived from the vernacular. Sunlight, scale, reminders of archetypal Kentucky houses, and an immediate sense of freedom combine to encourage communication with the stored experience of the users.

Contextual relevance to the life experiences of the occupants is a value of regional architecture that has been all but lost because of prevailing attitudes toward technology. An artful utilization of the visual cues from specific environments of the past may play an important role in forming a healthful climate for the mind. The main doctrines of modern architecture have ignored this possibility and have made only superficial use of our expanding knowledge of psychology and perception.

# 13 ACTS OF EXPERIENCE

*Dominican Monastery at La Tourette, near Lyon. L-C made his design develop from the horizontal terrace-roof—a grand all-commanding horizontal. Beneath it, are a hundred monks' cells and, below these, are rooms for study and meditation, while lower still are the refectories. At the bottom, partly touching the ground, are the kitchens. The structure is thus linked to the ground by pilotis. The cloister, cruciform, leads to the church, which is in modest rough concrete without moldings. Thin bands of light are arranged horizontally and vertically, and "canyons of light" stream down upon the monks at their worship from the highest point of the church, or enter from the side to bathe in brilliance the crypts where mass is celebrated in silence.*

Le Corbusier, *Creation Is a Patient Search*

The various human activities that are carried out in a particular building are an important source of imagery for a designer. Activities may be revealed and their significance heightened by the use of metaphor—that is, by the use of forms, materials, and spatial sequences that identify the activities by metaphoric allusions. In this way the final matrix to which the beholder responds may include references to his personal experiences that extend far beyond the limits of his ordinary perception of a particular type of activity. These experiences supply the principal routes for the participatory emotions as the attention is transferred from the "Now and Here" of the building itself to the "Then and There" of the layers of personal experience that are called up by the metaphor.

As an example, consider Le Corbusier's monastery La Tourette (fig. 50). In this building the architect dramatizes the individual cells of the monks as places for solitude and silence. From the exterior the cells are defined by very heavy, thick, concrete sidewalls and railings. It is almost impossible for the imagination not to conceive of experiences of caves and fortresses, experiences touched off by their association with those of monks. The caves are in the sky, adding ambiguity and mystery as the mind mingles layers and categories of experience. The cells are contrasted with library and dining spaces directly below, where the fenestration is of another kind, rhythmically varied and indicating a communal activity behind. Contributing to the poetic contrasts of this building is the completely

50. Le Corbusier's Monastery of Sainte-Marie-de-la-Tourette, 1956-59
*(G. E. Kidder Smith)*

open space from grass to parapet between the introverted form of the chapel and the cloister of cells. This open space, linking the interior court with the open landscape beyond, speaks of freedom and connection with the outside world, perhaps in a reference to the monk's retreat as an act of free will. At any rate the feelings of the protected, cavelike cloister are juxtaposed with feelings of freedom in an image of great dramatic impact.

For many architects La Tourette has provided a model that retains certain classical predispositions for form while freely responding to demands of function and usage. The top of the building is uniform and articulated; it gives the feeling of symmetry, echoing dimly, but with sure traces, ancient origins in Greece and Rome. In the lower levels varied spacing of columns allows a variety of functional and aesthetic treatments. It is unfortunate that architects seem to have been influenced only by the classical visual cues and to have missed the eloquence of form, materials, and spaces as they speak to us about the activities that are carried out within the building.

A ceremony attempts to stabilize thoughts and feelings so that they can be made to recur. One of the more ceremonial acts associated with architecture is that of entering a building. The stepped temples of Uxmal and the encompassing colonnade of St. Peter's are alike in that they place great significance on the ceremonial act of making an entrance. A problem for modern architecture is that meaningful ceremonies are sometimes difficult to establish. Modern society has lost interest in the ceremonies of religion and royalty, and few architects are prepared to seek new forms of ceremony in a society that seems uncertain what values it wants to stabilize.

In Le Corbusier's apartment block at Nantes-Rezé we find an interesting modern example of a dramatized entrance. In this building the fourteen hundred inhabitants cross a single bridge—six feet wide and fifty feet long—as the only means of entrance into the building. A bridge is a symbol of assistance given to man, a metaphor of overcoming obstacles. Since it must serve fourteen hundred inhabitants this bridge is also a symbol of communion. The ceremony of crossing the bridge is certainly low-key and capable of diverse interpretations. Perhaps some of the inhabitants have not made use of these symbolic resources. Yet they are available if the inhabitants choose to use them.

Another use of a bridge to dramatize experience is found in the theater project already described (figs. 26-27). A design aim here was to reveal the theater as a workshop for the creation of drama and illusion. The expression of this aim is facilitated by routing the audience through a transparent enclosed passage made of trusses filled in with glass. The passage acts as a connecting bridge from the entrance, past workshops and buildings for rehearsal, to the main theater space. If desired, operations in the shops can be revealed to the audience. The transparent bridge passes over a courtyard and extends to the opaque, win-

dowless mass of the theater. A dramatic transition is made between the real world of courtyard and cityscape and the imagined world of the theater.

The metaphor of a bridge is also developed in a project for the studio residence of a jazz pianist-turned-sculptor (figs. 51, 52). The site is a rolling Kentucky Bluegrass farm of twenty-five acres with a small grove of locust and beech trees. Tobacco barns with galvanized metal roofs can be seen on adjoining farms. The house is conceived as a bridge connecting the grove of trees with the studio, which stands in the cleared field. A grove of trees is rich with symbolic resources. By the gentle extension of the house into the grove, the user is brought into closer contact with these resources. Situated in the open field, the studio provides the user with natural vistas of the site, varied sources of natural light, and a protected outdoor space in which to work or to unload materials.

Among the owner's requirements were spaces for two grand pianos, walls for displaying works of art, and a continuous open living space with built-in furniture. He wanted the house to give a sense of being close to nature but at the same time comfortably apart from it. The floor of the living space above descends in seat-high increments to the pianos. The floors, walls, and ceiling are finished entirely in strip-oak flooring. The wood has acoustical advantages as does the shape of the room, which is without parallel walls. The bridge allows the user a dramatic descent into the grove of trees. At the same time the

51.  Elevation of Greene's studio-residence project, 1967

52.  Section of Greene's studio-residence project

stepped floor provides seating for an audience and stages for the pianos.

Another kind of dramatic entrance is seen in figures 53 and 54. This small four-story house was designed for an art professor who desired a dwelling that would have affinities with the Oklahoma Prairie House. A modest budget and a beautifully wooded site were among the factors that contributed to the vertical arrangement of living spaces. The first level, half in the ground, is given over to five young children. The second contains the living room, dining room, kitchen, and an outdoor deck. On the third level are master bedroom, spare bedroom, and balcony, while the fourth provides a study, sewing room, and a roof terrace up in the trees. The entrance is made into a stair tower affording visual contact with the trees and grounds and with the public spaces of the house. The stair, detailed to allow maximum transparency, is confined within the tower form with its shaftlike narrowness and totemic symmetry. But a sense of freedom is provided by the transparency, which enables one to see through the building to the trees beyond, and warmth of texture and color is given by the wood construction. The upward thrust of the tower and the close contact with the unusually fine trees outside provide resources that can help produce almost a religious experience. As the only means of circulation between levels, the narrow passage unites a family of seven. Since the budget did not allow for expenditures beyond the enclosure of space, the architec-

53. Greene's Furchess residence, 1968 *(Harry Furchess)*

54. Greene's Furchess residence *(Harry Furchess)*

103

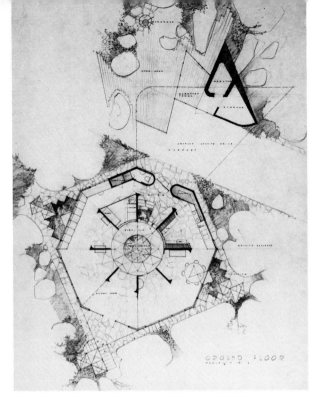

55. Plan of Greene's Joyce residence, 1958-59

ture of the entrance is part of the interior. However, as one approaches the tower from the outside, one can see into it and comprehend its form. Thus the symbolism of the tower becomes part of the act of entrance.

A variation on the theme of dramatizing the entrance may be seen in the Joyce house (figs. 55-58). In this house the act of "coming home"—approaching the house and entering into it—became important largely because of the site. The house is situated on a bluff of granite boulders, visible for miles along prairie approaches. The image presents an aspect of receptiveness, something to come home to.[1] The visual cues are the shingled form that opens up at the two-story living room, an accommodating posture, hovering and protective, and the tower on top (for mechanical equipment), which acts as a beacon. One side of the pyramidal tower is made of chunk glass that enables the tower to be seen as a low-wattage lighthouse.

One arrives under a broad, seven-foot-high carport, also serving as a roof terrace accessible from the upper level of the house. Visual contact with the site is maintained, but human qualification of scale is introduced. The sense of a place of arrival is established. Entrance is gained through a glass door five feet wide. The view is across the center of the house where there is a pool and fountain of polished granite, above which are stair landings sculptured to hold hanging plants. The arrangement of the two-story interior is revealed and the two-story glass wall beyond

104

56. Section of Greene's Joyce residence

the fountain provides views of the prairie one has just traversed.

The noted Philadelphia architect Louis Kahn has said that a window is a place.[2] Kahn was interested in the masonry architecture of ancient Rome, and when one considers the place made by the three-dimensional window void in the thick walls of Roman times, one can see a source of his aphorism. The importance of places is that human acts can happen in them and that they afford a perceptual complexity to which the significance of acts can be attached. Projecting window bays, for instance, can be desirable extensions of the spaces they adjoin. One can stand in them and enjoy the feeling of human scale and the sense of the body extending or pushing out. By placing objects and furnishings in the bays we can make these spaces especially our own.

In the Ward house (figs. 59, 60) it was our intention to design each window so that the activities carried out in the space behind the window would be implied or at least dramatized by its form. The varied details of placement, size, and configuration often become visual cues to call up experiences associated with the activities. For instance, dining is dramatized by a large window that is continued in the roof plane to form a skylight over the dining table. A window in a study is part of a built-in desk. A two-story window in a breakfast nook reveals a family room on a balcony above. The living room has two windows projecting into the wooded site. One has a window seat long enough for a person to

57. Exterior of Greene's Joyce residence *(Julius Shulman)*

58. Interior of Greene's Joyce residence *(Bob Bowlby)*

105

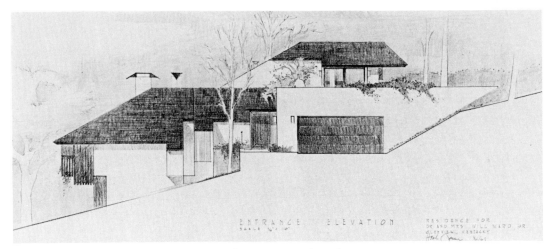

59. Elevation of Greene's Ward residence, 1970

recline on, while the other is designed for a group of house plants.

As well as being a place, a window can be an element suggesting anthropomorphic content with which the human being can identify in the same way he identifies with human scale and body metaphor in a building. Windows are the "eyes" of a building, or in buildings sheathed in glass, windows are the building's "skin." In the Prairie House (fig. 13) a window becomes a "place" by funneling the shape of the house down to an intimate size. It is also a Cyclopean eye balefully looking out at the world. The window sill is flush with a nine-by-five-foot built-in seat or bed. The window becomes a place for conversation with others, oneself, or with the distant horizon. More than one visitor has remarked that it looks like a place to make love. I did not have that act in mind when I designed it, but I can recognize a mild sense of "making an offering" in the arrangement, and sensuality can be read into the surrounding warm colors and some of the shapes and rhythmic patterns.

The first hundred years of modern architecture have been principally devoted to the expression of technological revolution and new aesthetic intentions. There are welcome indications that the next hundred years of architecture will consider the act of experience, both communal and individual, as a primary generator of significant form. The recent Galleria dormitory street, containing shops, residences, and recreation for students at the

106        60. Exterior of Greene's Ward residence *(Bill Strode)*

University of Alberta, is indicative of this concern (fig. 61). That the concept of form generated by social acts is not new we can perceive from examining the pueblos of Mesa Verde (fig. 62), which haunt us still with an image of an urban theater more integral with life than any dramatic setting in our own cities. Electronic communications notwithstanding, we feel the need for the experiences of communicative acts as embodied in the architecture of the pueblos, and in the architecture of the future we may find this need answered.

62. Mesa Verde *(National Park Service)*

61. Diamond and Myers's Galleria Housing Union Building, University of Alberta, 1970-72 *(John Fulker)*

# 14  METAPHOR

*A metaphor is not language, it is an idea expressed by language, an idea that in its turn functions as a symbol to express something. It is not discursive and therefore does not really make a statement of the idea it conveys; but it formulates a new conception for our direct imaginative grasp.*

Susanne K. Langer, *Problems of Art*

We can know objects only by seeing them in terms of our knowledge of other things, using metaphor as a tool for understanding. Metaphor, the transfer of references from one object to another, is also the bedrock of imagination, and image makers cannot function without its support. The most prosaic of us recognizes the grammar school variety of metaphoric language: a round, smiling face may be said to be "sunny"; a book has "leaves"; time may "flow"; thoughts "leap." The bisociative act and the use of codes and strategies are essential to a metaphoric transaction, though most of us are unconscious of these processes even while they occur.

In the plastic arts, we often participate in what might be called partial metaphors—metaphors that are not completed because of lack of information, loss of attention, or, in some cases, because of transmutation into new metaphors after further evaluation of the data. For instance, we can be aware that the columns in La Tourette (fig. 50) have affinities with legs before we need to make a state-ment to that effect. In a context with the "legs" and other parts of the image, the windows have affinities with eyes. But other meanings, set up by the relationship between the columns, second story, and top row of windows, distract us from seeing that metaphor through. Some meanings are familiar, some are new, as if we are discovering them for the first time. The cell-like cloister of the upper stories juxtaposed against the "open and free" of the tier of columns points to a new meaning, at least for me.

Whether *metaphor* is the best name for the process of seeing one thing in terms of other things, I am not sure. Both the word and the process have acquired negative reputations with many artists and art theoreticians in recent times. Our age has seen the development of abstract expressionism and of so-called pure design, which is asserted to be based on or to symbolize nothing but itself. A resistance has arisen against the idea that an object or an art expression can refer to the past and yet be uniquely itself in the present.

109

While it would seem an obvious contradiction to say that human expression could be divorced from past experience and still remain expression, we must remember that our age is still reacting against the stereotypes of the cloying and far-fetched symbolism of the nineteenth century.

Another reason for the low status of metaphor is a trend in the development of language. Susanne Langer points out that physical references, being more easily standardized than the metaphoric meanings, have come to monopolize the public meanings of words. This shift, she feels, has tended to obscure the role of metaphor in perception and learning.[1] The precision of expression gained by language when metaphorical meanings are given up is undoubtedly useful in certain forms of communication and in formulating scientific and mathematical concepts. But as a testament of the actual transaction between a perceived object and our mental experience, "literal language" gives a thin account, just as "pure design" would.

In order to understand the role of metaphor in apprehending or creating an image, we must remember that for the scanning mechanisms of the mind, an object is not a mere name with a single meaning. Instead it is a disposition of many cues. Cues for a table, for instance, may include flatness, color, a glossy reflection, generously rounded corners and edges, and so forth. Each of these cues, grasped in some unifying gestalt, is capable of initiating a metaphoric response. For example, the rounded edges of a table (if the radii are large enough) may be seen in terms of softness or of other objects that are soft. Situational or contextual conditions relating to the table also enter into the realization. These conditions might include a particular perspective that could give the table the appearance of being tied to the floor or, in contrast, of floating above it. The mental orientation of the beholder is also an important influence in the perception of objects. To an interior designer, Miës van der Rohe's famous glass table floats, cantilevered in perfect equilibrium from the thinnest possible chromed steel legs. To an aged pensioner used to Grand Rapids solidity, the glass table may seem unsteady. While we receive a complex of cues from the object and its contextual situation, it is by attitude and habit that we screen out some cues and accept those that fit our conception of what is important about the object. A person who rarely thinks of a table in any other way than as an object upon which to set dinner plates is unlikely to conceptualize it as a floating, transparent plane. Yet even in his evaluation of a table as an object upon which to set dinner plates, he must coordinate cues in the object such as horizontality, stability, size, and texture. Such coordination relies on seeing these features in terms of other things, even though the cues of the table have become routinely accepted as those of an object of use rather than of aesthetic contemplation.

It has been pointed out that during perception remembrance of past experiences may be stimulated by some visual cue of an object.

The particular experiences that are called to mind by a perceptual cue are different from the perceived object, of course, yet because of some similarity to the object, it is these particular experiences that are elicited. This "different yet like" relation of object to experience can be regarded as the substrate of metaphor. The advertising world more and more frequently presents us with images in which objects have been manipulated so that certain of their cues and contexts will produce a predictable response. Politicians and cans of shaving cream either do or are made to do things in television commercials in order to attract attention and to create metaphors that are supposed to add excitement to a personality or to an uninspiring product. This technique can be used for purposes more generous than either political or commercial advantage; the artist and the architect are able to direct metaphorical response to produce the interest and pleasure that give objects aesthetic value.

A single image may contain numerous metaphors, and the right combination of metaphors can greatly increase its complexity value and emotional power. Each new metaphor increases the wealth of experience available to be drawn upon as mental conceptions, or matrices, are cross-referenced and regrouped, activating layers of experience extending below or beyond the level of verbalization.

We can get some idea of the force of these preverbal levels of experience when we note the difference between actually experiencing an image that includes metaphor and simply talking about the metaphor. In La Tourette, for example, the image activates matrices contributing to such concepts and feelings as those of strength, mass, rhythm, thrust, and protection. These matrices, largely preverbal, perform deeper integrations of experience than does the mind when it is satisfied by the semantically distinct ideas arising from the expression "monastic cave" in reference to La Tourette or "house-buffalo" in reference to the Prairie House. The verbal juxtapositions may, in fact, seem quite incongruous, but on preverbal levels, harmonized concepts and feelings may arise from our confrontation with the diverse metaphoric matrices.

It should be noted that metaphoric associations are guided by both conscious and unconscious motivations. The context or situation of a perceived object may play a role in supplying direction to the associations, as in the example of the "buffalo" house on the plains of Oklahoma. The most important guidance, however, comes from frames of reference found in the image itself. The variations of form and fenestration expressive of the program of a monastery, the plastic expression of volume and void, and the historical references of La Tourette, or the psychological tone of the Prairie House, suggest strategies that influence the beholder's interpretation of the various details of the image. Interrelationships among the forms of the details of an image, or harmonies, provide common members for the different metaphors and supply direction to the concepts and feelings elicited by the image. Harmonies are essential both for the aesthetic consistency of the image and for its comprehension. Extending far beyond the mere relationship of shapes, harmonies arise out of the use of related forms, proportions, and other sense data to call up compatible meanings from a diversity of possibilities; they guide the selection of strategies by which we appropriate some meanings and dismiss others when we are stimulated by the diverse references in an image. For instance, the harmonies of proportion, material, and form in the "leg" columns and the "cave" windows of La Tourette assist us to dismiss incompatibilities and to find consistencies between legs and caves.

The theories of organism emphasize the importance to the artist of the psychological field and the dismantled stored mental experience called into play during a perceptual act. Instead of expecting the intellect to recognize an image that supposedly represents an ideal type, the organic approach aims at increasing the participation of the beholder by drawing upon his reservoir of stored experience. The Prairie House illustrates an organic approach to images in that it consciously incorporates a variety of metaphors. The image involves the metaphors in varying degrees of definiteness and overlap: the form that might be a house, as signaled by enveloping and rooflike shingled surfaces, has a window that overcomes its reference to some kind of eye or orifice by becoming a place for people.[2] The sense of a dwelling is established by the protecting roof, the human scale, the warm color, the cue of seating or bed in the window, and certain rhythmic patterns. The creaturelike metaphors apparent in the image cannot easily be verbalized, but they include impressions of a large object—a thing or creature—rather at home on or accommodating itself to an expanse of natural prairie, sheltering itself with its coat or its feathers. Gentleness, power, and a state of being wounded or of vulnerability are suggested.

The universality of a great many physiological sensations and cultural experiences produces some agreement about the meaning of certain symbols and images; but the particular life experiences of individual human beings vary, particularly in their translation into verbal concepts. Thus it is natural that some people find metaphors in the image other than those mentioned above. The intention of the design is not so much to make explicit references as it is to supply whole frames of reference, such as gentleness, power, shelter, and creaturehood, into which the percipient may read his own experience. Some people see more fish than fowl in the image of the Prairie House.

Contradictions and ambiguities produced by metaphors are not necessarily chaotic. The designer seeks ways to include diversities in an image and to unify them, because in an organic world any element ultimately requires connection with its opposite to reach fullness of meaning. One can feel the necessity of the tensive contrasts in the inky blackness of a Turner ship next to the milky whiteness of an adjoining sky, or in the closed spaces of the cells of La Tourette above the openness of the ground level. The image of La Tourette is haunted by a feeling of the irony of knowing that in order to reveal the character of what a monastery is, the image must include statements of what a monastery is not.

In the design process of the Joyce residence (figs. 55-58) metaphoric imagery was cultivated from the earliest contact with the design situation, but not within a particular logical sequence. Metaphoric ideas may begin as response to site, environment, users or owners themselves, building materials, or to the construction strategies anticipated. It is necessary to remain flexible, to discard some ideas in favor of others that seem more promising. The principles of architecture require that function be understood before a physical expression to house that function is derived. Thus it should not be necessary to sacrifice solutions to practical problems for the sake of imagery. Indeed practical necessities often become the catalysts for the development of imagery: solutions to the problems of sun control, roof drainage, or zoning for family uses may suggest images or alter strategies for obtaining images. The Joyce residence was initially conceived as a two-story mass, somewhat indefinite as to form and details, and it was only to meet the problem of sun control for the extensive glass of the lower story that the particular roof overhang took shape. It was then that the opportunity for its brim- or winglike form was recognized, and the dominant visual cue for the hovering metaphor of

the house was established in that process.

Several bird metaphors are operating in this house. The cues are the winglike roof overhang, the lack of visible support for the mass of the roof, and, perhaps, the downspout that Mrs. Joyce refers to as the house's tail feathers. A hovering, thrusting image is produced, projecting messages of freedom, flight, and spirit. The molded plaster undersides of the overhangs are "different yet like" the soft, feathered undersides of ducks. The quality of softness plays a role similar to that of human scale: the softness tells us that an aspect of the building is like us.

The metaphor of a geode is also present. The architect has sometimes been fascinated by objects in nature that are at first contact unpleasant but gradually become interesting and even pleasing after inspection and acquaintance. This kind of transformation occurs when one breaks open a geode. The formation seems an apt symbol of the often deceptive relationship between appearance and reality.

One response to symbolic objects derives out of the mind's understanding of the adventures of such objects in the world. Recognition of how the usual feelings attached to the objects arose, awareness of what the objects are in their intrinsic nature, anticipations of their future—such thoughts exert influences on the strategies we use in valuing one object in comparison with another. Thus the softness and protectiveness of the feathers of birds, their capability of flight, their beautiful shapes that we often transform into symbols

113

63. Exterior of Eero Saarinen's John Deere Headquarters, 1957-63 *(Deere and Co.)*

of spirit, and the blindness of their consciousness as compared to human awareness influence me to work with birds rather than with soup cans; I feel a greater empathy with the phenomenal and historical adventures of birds.

Metaphor rarely enters into the explicit design process of modern architects who plan large corporate and civic prospects, but this rule has notable exceptions as shown by certain buildings of the late Eero Saarinen. In the headquarters of the John Deere Company, located in Moline, Illinois, appear metaphors with specific references to the products of a large corporation (figs. 63, 64). Eero Saarinen wrote of this building group: "We had three major intentions in planning and designing these buildings. First, to provide functional, efficient space which would take care of future expansion in flexible ways. Second, to create the kind of pleasant and appropriate environment for employees which is part of Twentieth Century thinking. And third, to express in the architecture the special character of Deere and Company.

"We tried to get into the buildings the character of John Deere products, the company and the customers it serves, and the friendly, informal attitude of its personnel."[3]

Rust-colored, weathering steel is assembled into elaborate sunshades to set up reminiscences of farm machinery. Saarinen pursued this approach to materials and form after a preliminary design in reinforced concrete was cooly received by the client. This might indicate that lay persons are sometimes more receptive to the use of metaphor than are most architects. The sunshades are compulsively extended to the north side of the building, contributing to the symmetry typical of contemporary office buildings; but the frankly associative use of materials and form, unique in a contemporary building of this size, suggests an approach to architecture in which characteristics and objects associated with the manufacture and merchandising of a particular group of products become ingredients in the image of the building that is to house these activities.

From these examples it can be seen that metaphor is a resource for enriching the interaction between the beholder and architecture. The designer, by including references and meanings that are recognized as belonging to realms of experience lying beyond the familiar and more literal meaning of the building, presents the beholder with the familiar placed in alternation with the unfamiliar. While a reference may be unfamiliar and its meaning in an image be surprising and even contradictory, it may nonetheless elicit valued knowledge and feeling. Metaphor can make us more sensitive to our ties with the phenomenal world and deepen our understanding of those ties.

64. Interior of Eero Saarinen's John Deere Headquarters  *(Deere and Co.)*

115

# 15 HUMAN SCALE, BODY METAPHOR, & RHYTHM

*This suggests a closer identification of rhythm as the causal counterpart of life; namely, that wherever there is some rhythm, there is some life, only perceptible to us when the analogies are sufficiently close. The rhythm is then the life, in the sense in which it can be said to be included within nature.... The essence of rhythm is the fusion of sameness and novelty; so that the whole never loses the essential unity of the pattern, while the parts exhibit the contrast arising from the novelty of their detail. A mere recurrence kills rhythm as surely as does a mere confusion of differences.*

Alfred North Whitehead, *Principles of Natural Knowledge*

In the organic approach to architecture, the most important determinant of form is lived experience of human beings. Since the human body is the vehicle for the expression of lived experience, it offers us a basic source of symbols to which significant experience can be attached. To create a psychologically satisfying environment, the organic architect tries to devise symbols that will enable us to reflect on and recover the valued experiences that can be associated with symbols of the bodily life. Human scale can be considered such a symbol. As an element in the environment it is of extreme importance.

Human scale can reflect our individual existential being. Its presence in the environment makes us feel "at home" and can encourage us to interact with the environment. One important psychological effect of human scale in an image is that the beholder feels the human being is in control of his environment. Human scale reveals that human action has been taken to make building materials into sizes man can handle. When man's dimensions are impressed into openings and other forms that suggest his presence, the sense of manageability and human intercession awakens feelings whose roots extend into the unconscious. Such feelings speak to us with messages that say the building is "like us," that it is "human."

Human scale can also evoke participatory emotions. It acts in concert with other data in an image—data that might be present in materials, objects, shapes, or spaces—to encourage a sense of shared human experience. The Mayan city of Uxmal, where concepts of heaven and earth are merged with societal concepts and human scale is suffused and reflected throughout the entire city, seems to me a particularly vivid example. The human proportions and the rhythmic tapestries of stone mosaic constantly send messages of human care and control in this environment of buildings and carefully composed spaces between buildings. The elements of human scale tell us on preverbal levels that the buildings are like us. A strong feeling of empathy with the buildings and spaces is produced, and yet the viewer is confronted with building shapes of massive proportion and great repose, reminding him of nearby mesas and mountains. The image mingles matrices of human scale with those of cosmic scale.

The modern architecture in which one feels the most affecting sense of human scale is probably that of Frank Lloyd Wright, partly because of his deep interest in this design principle. No other architect of his extraordinary gifts has written, talked, or preached so much about the meaning of human scale or has been at such pains to establish it in his work. It is true that many tight spaces appear in his buildings—stairways two feet wide, unusable toilets, and head-bumping eaves; Wright was short in stature and designed his buildings in response to his own size. But more important, Wright was strong in the belief that he was the apostle of a revelation about architecture. One message of that revelation was that no matter how large, small, or complex works of architecture are, no matter what the source of ideas for the form, every visible part should reflect human dimensions.

The consciousness of this idea above all others is manifest in Wright's work.

When we compare the way scale is used in Wright's work with the way it was used in Mitla (fig. 65), it is evident that there can be more to scale than size and proportion alone. The exquisite palace at Mitla, dating from about A.D. 900, looks as if it might have been designed by Wright. It has that amplitude and power of form so surprising to see in the diminutive proportions one discovers upon drawing close to it. It also has the horizontal lines, geometric forms, integral ornament, and sense of fit to land that are characteristic of Wright. But in Wright's work, size qualifies expressions of form and materials so that we are reminded of man as a free individual rather than as a unit submerged in a social group. It is the vision of adapting human scale to specific situations and to various materials and methods that is unique in Wright. By responding to the individual situation, his work suggests freedom combined with a creative intelligence that comes to terms with the situation for the benefit of the individual. In the Millard house (fig. 39), for instance, the patterns in the concrete blocks express many things besides human scale: they are a conscious reference to the transparencies and verticality of the foliage of the site; they communicate an awareness of the nature of concrete and its ability to be accommodated to a mold; they also reveal how the walls are made into a continuous structural and ornamental tapestry, with a sense of showing how things work that a Da Vinci might enjoy.

Wright's preferences for warm colors and materials and his elaborate play of light and shade enrich his spaces with suggested meanings that seem wholesome and profound. He creates a chiaroscuro that can suggest a complexity greater than that of mere dimension. The end result in Wright's works, even in buildings where the user has few comfortable places to sit or suitable walls on which to hang pictures, gives a sense of the individual presiding over a complex of forces and events. It is, I think, the most fundamental message contributed by Wright's scale, reflecting a very different quality from that of many recent government buildings, which by their great size and their monotonous facades, altogether lacking in human scale, suggest the subordination of the individual to an external authority.

Human scale may be considered a metaphor of the body projected into the environment. Architects representing most of the current ideologies acknowledge its value. The consideration of body metaphors other than human scale for architecture, however, remains an undeveloped topic. The human sense of the vertical, human centering, human balance, and human gesture rarely enter into the conscious trains of reasoning used in determining architectural forms; yet the "stance" of La Tourette (fig. 50) and the balance and gesture of the cantilevers of Falling Water (Wright's historic work for Edgar Kaufmann) offer vivid evidence of the value of body metaphor as a means by which we can establish signs of humanness in a building.

65. Palace at Mitla *(Philip Welch)*

119

We have pointed out that in La Tourette the columns supporting the projecting mass above are like legs. It is a nuance that contrasts with the feeling of the powerful geometric forms. In Falling Water vertical masses of stone and the horizontal cantilevers of concrete slabs and balconies suggest human gestures. The vertical gesture of the tallest pier, as it appears to one looking up at the building from the stream below, seems to touch our experience of gaining a sense of vertical balance and reflects a physical sense of aspiration. The "reaching out" of the balconies can be read with some of the same interpretations as the reaching out of a human being can—that is, as gestures of assertion, welcome, or orientation. The inclusion of metaphors of the body seems to me to be of the utmost significance in establishing an environment that reveals its human origin and thus its humanness, but a drive through a metropolis of the 1970s shows what a minority viewpoint this is. The primary metaphor of most office buildings seems to be that of a filing cabinet. I do admit that creating a context for body metaphor or any other metaphor is a delicate matter; merely projecting balconies in all directions is not advocated. But the artistic use of body metaphor can be a powerful reminder of valued bodily experience.

Body metaphor includes a sense of "bodying forth," to use the parlance of existentialists. In bodying forth, the self projects itself by means of the body. The term implies gesture but also carries the suggestion of an intention to act. I believe the Prairie House includes an element of bodying forth. The element is produced within a matrix of metaphors that suggests a living creature that hovers, looks, listens, and possesses a capacity for action.

Body metaphor is an important element by which architecture can be humanized, and perhaps the most important body metaphor is rhythm. The fundamental importance of rhythm in an image is that it communicates to us a sense of what it is to be alive. As an element projected into the environment it allows us to acknowledge our understanding of the rhythms that characterize the world. From molecules to planets, from cells to complex organisms, nature is characterized by rhythm.

Rhythm is the result of change. It suggests that the consummation of one phase is the preparation for another. Although repeating cycles characterize rhythm, the unchanging exact repetition that is sometimes thought of as its essence is here considered to be a special case, one that is not apt as a characterization of the dynamic interplay among most of the acts and functions of higher organisms. The complexity and numbers of rhythms brought into play in an act are often beyond the powers of our observation. The ballet dancer's movements, for example, involve so many large and small rhythms that we learn to devote our attention to some of the most visible. In the dance we are impressed with those rhythms that possess high metaphoric content, yet these symbolic rhythms also reflect the substrate of rhythms found in bodily tissues, organs, and even in psychic moods whose cycles lie below our conscious awareness.

We do not tolerate mere repetition in an image any more than nature tolerates it in the world. Exact repetition cannot exist in life because growth and change are essential parts of being alive. Yet if we are under the influence of aesthetic codes that place high value on symmetry and uniformity we can minimize the need for rhythm in an image. These codes have channeled much Western architecture into forms like that of the Bienecke Library (fig. 66). Many people admire the Bienecke, and this fact would seem to indicate widespread approval of the reduction of rhythmic contrast, especially in a context of the classical elegance connoted by white marble. But whether one responds positively to the image or feels, like Vincent Scully, that it produces alienation in the viewer, it is a relatively small building set within an urban context of variety and contrast.[1] Within such a context, the Bienecke as a unit becomes an element of rhythmic change. However, when we look at huge blocks of new office buildings in Manhattan, as we do in the vicinity of the Time-Life Building near Sixth Avenue, we can feel a deadness and monotony, since there is no larger context for contrast and escape.

An eloquent scientist, René Dubos, after admitting that the threats to human needs most easily identified are those resulting from physiochemical and biological factors in the environment, goes on to say that influences affecting human life cannot always be mea-

66. Skidmore, Owings and Merrill's Bienecke Rare Book and Manuscript Library, Yale University, 1963 *(Yale University News Bureau)*

121

67. Greene's Moorman residence project, 1963

sured in terms of chemicals, decibels, and population statistics.[2] Man converts external stimuli into symbols and commonly responds to the symbols rather than to the actual stimuli. One wonders what kind of symbolic quality will finally emerge from the rhythmless, scaleless monoliths of Sixth Avenue. Obviously, many people see them as signs of economic growth and technological progress and find them acceptable by popular standards of styling. It is my view, however, that because these structures do not meet man's need for an architecture of rhythm and scale, further evaluation will show that they produce feelings of alienation. Although alienation is difficult to measure, much of it seems already to have developed.

In images, as in nature, rhythm occurs most obviously as the expression of a change of function. Therefore, the articulation of changes in function gives opportunities for

the creation of rhythms in architecture. The rhythmic articulation of a change of function alone, however, does not satisfy our urge to seek some sense of guiding purpose. This urge is again based on our experience of nature, which usually sees rhythm connected with causality and purpose, whether in growth, tidal cycles, or birdsong. Thus, for strong links with experience, rhythm must be combined with reference frames and metaphors that are organized to demonstrate purpose.

Figure 67 is an elevation drawing of a project for a house on the plains of Oklahoma. The site is a tilting, rolling prairie, often planted in wheat or straw-colored winter grass that undulates in the wind. The project was to be an economical version of a wooden frame and shingle house. The image suggests shelter by the use of walls that slope at angles and express mass. These walls also express changes of function: they vary in width to accommodate the bedrooms, closets, and baths behind them, and some of them are formed into sun shades. The slope of the walls increases progressively and forms a rhythmic sequence moving against the horizon. The projections of the walls allow ventilation at either horizontal or vertical returns, so that the view windows need not open. The articulation of the sloped walls forms a deep shadow and suggests a wing or flap. A secondary illusion of the house is that it is freeing itself from the ground. The rhythmic articulations help to express these metaphors. The sunshade walls amplify the metaphor of a stretching out to the horizon and add to the sense of protection conveyed by the image. The end result is a rhythmic statement with a suggestion of purpose arising out of the cue of accumulating masses interacting with the secondary illusions of flight and protection.

In a residence by George Muennig (fig. 68), the structure of undulating two-by-six-inch wood members provides rhythms that may be associated with the living and the lifelike. The frame of reference that links life and form is that of continual change. Within the undulating surface an individual member may be perceptually grasped as an individual detail that contributes to a sense of life and motion. The progression of members seems to limit and define the interior space and at the same time to lead beyond it, providing a sense of freedom from an explicit enclosure. The rhythmic progressions developed by this form suggest a visual model of Whitehead's characterization of the basic physical situation as a

68. Interior of residence by George Muennig, Joplin, Missouri, 1965 *(Bob Bowlby)*

123

vibratory ebb and flow.[3] The resulting form of Muennig's design also seems to me to integrate structure, mass, and ornament into an expression that is distinguished by its continuity and its unity. A sameness of quality pervades every aspect of the form, springing from the same source of feeling.

If a combination of rhythms can be harmonized in an image, the result is like a dialogue or conversation in which one rhythm informs, supports, or offers contrasts to the other. The value of rhythmic dialogues is that they allow and encourage us to organize complex groups of contrasts much in the manner of orchestration in music.

In the interior of the Prairie House (fig. 69) there are several rhythmic systems in dialogue. One is in the shingled walls; another consists of the lines formed by the intersections of walls, floors, and ceiling; a third is provided by the stairway. The walls are covered with wood shingles. They speak of human scale, warmth, softness, and vibratory activity. They suggest feathers, scales, nests, baskets, ebb and flow, and life and motion. The lines made by intersecting surfaces suggest animate gestures and give a feeling of recovering one's balance with the vertical. The lines lead inward and then outward, as they close the space and open it. The stairway presents a contrast of "the straight away" with the surrounding curves. It also sets up contrasts to the sense of enclosure one reads into the space. We feel that there is an escape, a place beyond.

69. Interior of Greene's Prairie House, 1962 *(Doug Kirkland)*

124

It has been asserted that all curves in architecture that are not structural are vicious. By this token much of Gaudí's Park Güell—including the famous tiled seating atop the colonnaded market—is vicious, and yet it would be difficult to think of an architect who is Gaudí's peer in the command of structure in the strictest tectonic sense. It is apparent that Gaudí was acutely sensitive both to life experiences and to the forms of nature as sources for design. His work employs an extensive system of references to the opening and closing of growing, living things. Caution must be used in intellectualizing upon specific metaphoric forms because the words used may contain unsuitable associations, while the meaning triggered by the actual assemblage of cues given in an image may touch and enrich deeply buried layers of stored experiences. Such enrichment stems from the contrasting frames of reference set up by cues in the image.

In the window of the Colonia Güell Chapel (fig. 70), the outstretched flower pattern and its white, blue, and yellow colors set up cheerful references in contrast to the less cheerful messages in the stonework surrounding the window. The reference to the animate in the stonework harmonizes with the characteristic free opening of the flower. The structural integrity of the masonry opening is maintained, but the final qualities of its shape issue not from structural demands but from stored experiences of the stretching and opening of living things. Additional frames of reference supplied by the visual cues—spirit, joy, or

70. Window of Antonio Gaudí's Colonia Güell Chapel, 1898-1915
*(Lucas Collins)*

125

radiance—suggest strategies that sublimate one's opening and closing codes associated with the orifices of animals. The expressive sublimations provide the mind with means to reenact important memories in a directed interplay. The image expresses a recognition of the process of evolution itself in its inclusion of growth, change, and living things in the matrices. Contrasts such as that between darkness and light in the context of Gaudí's image also allow for the antecedents of the feelings that are triggered by these visual cues to become part of the matrix.

Gaudí's window illustrates an organic approach to architecture in that his image uses cues of the existential and phenomenal experiences of organisms. Lifelike curves, such as appear in Gaudí's work, are not the only kinds of lifelike references; and we do not advocate the wholesale use of literal analogies to organic life in the shapes and textures of architecture. The use of particular forms in images, like the use of particular words in conversation, is subject to the changing outlooks and intentions of society and its artists. In making analogies with the lifelike, it is the designer's double problem to find the appropriate form to refer to and to determine the degree of abstraction that is most fitting to a particular design situation. However, there is no more justification for legislating against analogies to the lifelike than there is for legislating against the images of machines. The image maker should be free to use whatever sources and means seem appropriate within a particular design situation. But it should be emphasized that the importance of the bodily experience is inescapable. Most modes of architecture fail to use that store of meanings on levels that reflect their true importance.

# 16 SYNTHESIS

*Among chosen combinations the most fertile will often be those formed of elements drawn from domains which are far apart. . . . Most combinations so formed would be entirely sterile; but certain among them, very rare, are the most fruitful of all.*

Henri Poincaré, *Mathematical Creation*

Discussions of the design process often seem fatuous or superficial, because many of the most important determinants for design remain hidden in the designer's unspoken and often unconscious presuppositions. The designer may favor the precepts of classicism or those of organism, or he may think of his task as one of environmental engineering. He may be influenced by controversial design issues such as the use of chance. He may have ingrained cultural and personal predispositions, and he may be subject to pressures from his environment either to maintain current norms or to seek some new concept. Since it is impossible to keep all of one's experiences and beliefs at the threshold of consciousness, some of the forces that affect design synthesis exert their influence at subconscious levels. Such influences are normal to the thinking process. Arthur Koestler speaks of "unconscious guidance" and discusses its contribution to problem solving in science and in art.[1]

The silence of the leading rationalist architects of the past sixty years on the topic of unconscious guidance has been almost com-plete. Certain historical reasons for this silence will be discussed in section 21, but it is to be noted that even today architectural academies rarely encourage preverbal, intuitive guidance in problem solving and design. In their desire for decisions based on the objective and the impersonal, they value primarily those concepts that can be quantified and verbalized at the upper limit of consciousness.

Before we discuss the process of synthesis in architectural design, let us consider the topic more generally. In painting and sculpture, more obviously than in most architecture, objects from the world about us often serve as matter for synthesis. We tend to "master" objects familiarized in the environment just as we master a skill; once this happens the objects have become stereotyped. In a successfully synthesized image, objects are freed of their stereotypes so that we can respond to the actual feelings and meanings they elicit within the framework of an image. A bicycle wheel was just a wheel until Du-champ placed one on a pedestal in an art

127

gallery and by so doing suggested that we could break the stereotype: we may ponder the completeness suggested by the circularity and symmetry of the wheel, for instance; or we may associate the intricate hub and thin radial spokes with the insect world; or we may feel suggestions of space and a great scale. It is likely that many of the feelings aroused by our contemplation of the wheel are responses to unconscious awareness of particular features of the image.

The twentieth century has seen an outburst of synthesis that relies on the placement of objects in unfamiliar contexts so that they are likely to lose their stereotypes and thus elicit new meaning. The synthesis that occurs is very much like the bisociative process in which self-consistent, but commonly incompatible, concepts are brought together. The resulting juxtaposition of the experiences associated with objects is aimed variously at poetic metaphor, humor, or shock value. The bicycle seat and handlebars made into an image of a bull by Picasso, the advertisement of a Volkswagen bus posed and painted to look like Superman, and the oversized soup can of pop art which surprises by a grossly magnified scale are examples of this kind of juxtaposition.

Le Corbusier overcame a stereotype and achieved dramatic synthesis of content in a crucifix designed for the Chapel of Our Lady at Ronchamp. By shortening the top and extending the horizontal member of a cross, he called upon an unfamiliar, yet lifelike, strain of the human form to revitalize the meaning of a symbol so familiar as almost to be stereotyped as a mere sign of the church.

In these examples the image incorporates or alludes to objects that have relatively long histories in human consciousness. Forgotten experiences of these objects may be recalled by a new juxtaposition. Past experiences of the objects are not the only ones evoked, however. The sense cue of the object may produce anticipations of yet-to-be-actualized experience. For instance, in figure 12 the juxtaposition of geometric loops, which can suggest rhythm and energy, with gestalts of the scales of creatures and of architectural materials can create anticipations of some yet-to-be-actualized architectural structure.

Turning to the synthesis of architectural images, we must recognize that several areas of problem solving and decision making interact to produce the final result. We need to distinguish between the solution of routine problems of function and building construction on the one hand and, on the other, the design processes that bring to bear the guiding dispositions that influence a designer toward a particular mode of expression. While both call for synthesis, in the solution of routine problems the synthesis is on a more conscious or intentional level.

In the designing of the Prairie House (frontispiece, figs. 13, 14), the architect's use of his knowledge of the structural properties of wood and his search for a form with minimal wind resistance were examples of routine synthesis. The structural possibilities of the light wood framing members of which the house was to be built suggested a construction strategy of curved forms. The very wide range of possibilities within this strategy was reduced by the simultaneous requirement that the form be wind resistant. A logical solution was a slender elliptical shape that would present a minimal target to Oklahoma storms, which usually approach from the southwest.

The construction and wind resistance factors that contributed to the form meshed with other determinants of the design situation, resulting in the synthesis of the existing form. In retrospect I can see that some of the determinants were consciously recognized and some were not. From the beginning the metaphor of a hovering creature or bird appealed to me on a conscious level. The prairie site, in an almost natural state with vast sky and untouched horizons, seemed to support the metaphor. A two-story diamond shape with sloping planes, which was an early conception of the design, gave way to the curves of an asymmetrical ellipse. The exterior sheath of shingles and boards could be made to relate to the specific forms of adjoining ravines and windblown grass and at the same time to define a multisymbolic form suggesting a range of things, from creature to mandala.

While I was consciously using the hovering-creature metaphor from the inception of the design, I was unaware of any disposition to incorporate the image of a wounded creature. The inclusion of this element was probably a result of my finding the opportunity in the situation of designing my own house to accommodate this kind of latent disposition.

One function of the unconscious seems to be that of keeping an issue constantly on the agenda even while conscious attention is elsewhere, thus providing a state of receptivity to unsuspected opportunities of solving the problems of synthesis. As one becomes familiar with the practical aspects of a design situation (such as the physical possibilities of manipulating rafters, shingles, and boards), ideas occur for accommodating one's guiding dispositions. Shingles and boards became the scales, feathers, and rhythms through which I could demonstrate my emerging thoughts and feelings about the expression of time through references to diverse orders of things. At the same point I began to visualize how gestalts of a wounded creature could be formed in the image.

The disposition for forms that could make the house into a "hovering creature" had a long history. What we refer to as free association is, of course, never free. Hidden motivations, often persisting over a lifetime, guide the choices of what one mingles together to produce a designed form. Such long-term motivations are revealed by the appearance of similar gestalts in images executed years apart. In a student project for a post office, executed in 1951 at the University of Oklahoma, the "hovering creature" is already apparent (fig. 71). Copper-clad roofs supported by steel trusses reach out to protect both the public drive-in entrance and the loading dock that receives and dispatches mail. Federal offices are located in the small structure that rises

129

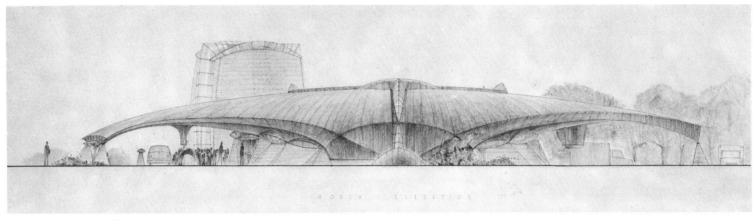

71. Greene's post office project, 1951

above. A "rising up" and a "settling down" are among the primary metaphors of the outstretched roof, and these are reinforced by the suggestion of mechanical or avian wings. These metaphors, which can obviously be related to a hovering creature, are tied into the disposition of the building so that it appears to be in a state of action or "doing," with stronger references to experiences of creature life than to the operations of machines. Related gestalts may be seen in the 1959 Joyce house (figs. 55-58). The resolutions of form in the Joyce residence and the Prairie House continue the dispositions established in the earlier image of the post office, even though conscious aims that could be attached to such a carry-over were negligible. The subconscious goal-directedness that would seem to be revealed by the repetition of the metaphors can be linked to the development of complexity values as discussed in section 7. It appears that both the "hovering creature" and "wounded" metaphors represented an attempt to express a reference to the living and sentient and to express a concept of time by suggesting diverse orders of things in the same image. Such an expression was valued more through intuition than through rational analysis. Only after the fact were rational and communicable goals attributed to certain elements of the expression.[2]

The designer's predisposition to use metaphoric gestalts that are significant to his own experience is among the limitations acknowledged by proponents of the organic approach to image synthesis. But whether the gestalts include metaphoric allusions to geometric forms, machines, the human body, or birds, the designer is alerted to include or delete them in response to the specific requirements of the user, site, and situation; his primary aim should always be to produce a form that is vividly expressive of these determinants.

Unity in organic synthesis results from the expression in each part of the design of the same view of the determinants of the design. Among the most important theorists of organic design synthesis was Louis Sullivan. His conception of architectural ornament as an expression of individual character and of unity of a particular type is still in advance of most present-day theory. Sullivan saw ornament as a requirement for fully developed architecture. In his view, the purpose of ornament is to heighten the expression of architectural structure and enclosure, amplifying and intensifying the qualities and ideas that determine the character of a space or of a mass.

The uplifting scallops on the coping and the radial bursts of the frieze on the Getty tomb (fig. 32) are ornamental qualifications of mass that seem expressive of joy, life, delicacy, and aspiration—in harmony with Sullivan's germinal idea of this tomb as an expression of the feminine and life-renewing. Sullivan's conception of the causality of form relies on an analogy to biological growth patterns: each separate part of the design repeats an aspect of the form and intention of the germinal idea.

The influence of Sullivan's notions of heightening the expression of architectural enclosure by the use of ornament is seen in some of the architectural examples in this book. The germinal idea generating the primary space is a synthetic response (limited by the designer's strategies of geometric expression) to user experience, building type, particular site, and other prominent features in the problem layout. The colors, textures, and forms derived from user experience that are used to qualify the primary space can be considered types of ornamental enrichment. They become symbols for the user and they contribute to the unity of the image, since each expressive element of texture or form is related to the character of the whole. Because the problem layout varies, particularly in the area of user experience, a distinctly different solution for each design situation necessarily results.

Rhythm also plays an important role in the organic approach to design. The rhythmic progressions in Sullivan's ornament act as organizational devices enhancing the expression of contrasts. Concurrent with the concept of a rhythmic organization runs an idea of the building as a continuous, plastic surface that maintains its integrity while changing to whatever functional or aesthetic form may be required. Sullivan expressed both continuity and change in works such as his banks, in which the ornamental enrichment seems to grow out of the mass of the buildings to culminate in one or more terminal events. This handling of ornament reminds one of paintings by Rembrandt in which a figure emerges from the ground with a powerful feeling of being connected to the ground and at the same time free to express individuality in its details.

131

Other principles of organic synthesis may be linked to terms derived from the writings of William James and Alfred North Whitehead. James described the world as "in the making."[3] Since architecture needs to show itself to be a part of the world, its images should impart a feeling that they are "in the making." Signs of a form in the making are likely to appear when architecture expresses movement and change and when it reveals clues of adaptation to specific sites, building materials, and user programs. The value of an image that appears to be in the making is that it provides a symbol of the change, growth, and decline we see in organic life around us.

From Whitehead comes the theory, continually used throughout this book, that an object of perception is not a fixed entity but a multiplicity of aspects, discernible to us by various cues of sense data that we measure against our own sensory, intellectual, and emotional experience.[4] Such a conception can free us from stereotyped thought about what a "bicycle seat" or a "house" is and offers possibilities for the reexamination of familiar objects and the creation of new ones. An important aspect of Whitehead's conception lies in the possibility of harmonizing apparently disparate or contradictory cues. I believe the Volkswagen bus advertisement would be successful only at a time when it is generally accepted that a powerful way to create meaning is to involve the audience in a process of harmonizing disparate phenomena. Whitehead's basis for harmony is a thoroughgoing acceptance of the idea of evolution—the idea that all the different entities in the world ultimately derive from the same original substance. This idea forces the recognition of real unity among all entities.

As an example of an architectural image synthesized in light of the dispositions of organic theory, let us consider the Joyce house (figs. 55-58). It is possible to trace some part of the process of adapting the dispositions of the designer to the exigencies of program, materials, and site, noting also, where feasible, the more philosophical influences on the image.

The Joyces wanted to build on a granite bluff near their quarry. They had discarded several designs prepared by other architects as being unsuited to the site and to their unusual collection of furnishings. They had a quantity of scrap granite from their quarry, and they suggested using it in the new house.

Several factors discouraged the use of the granite for the walls of the house. The cost would be high and the practical problems great. And while I disliked the idea of a formal, symmetrical granite house among the large boulders of the natural site, on the other hand, an asymmetrical granite form, irregular and informal, would have been out of character with the owners' personal objects and orderly life-style. Moreover, the unrestricted views that the site made desirable were more fully attainable with the use of a lighter, more plastic material. Thus it was decided to make the walls of wood and glass, reserving the granite for the floor. The floor became a massive pedestal to place the house firmly on the site and to display the users' furniture. The sides of the pedestal slope to the ground at an angle of forty-five degrees, repeating the angle of the overhanging sun shade. The pedestal's sense of "firm anchor" contrasts with the floating roof above.

Among the users' possessions were Swedish heirlooms, heavy Victorian furniture, eighteenth-century rococo chairs, white porcelains, and brass and crystal chandeliers. The overflow from their house then filled three small barns and included stained-glass windows, carved woodwork from a confessional booth, a backbar from an old hotel, and ornamental iron gates.

It seems clear that the attention and attitude of the beholder of an object determine what shall be a stimulus for him and what shall not. To an architect holding to his share of contemporary dogmas, these objects were at first not a stimulus. They were seen through his stereotyped codes that tended to deny the value of the "old-fashioned." There were mitigating circumstances, however. The owners enjoyed their objects; they stored and handled them with loving care. They had a splendid site on a granite bluff overlooking flat grasslands, distant from other buildings. Another important advantage was the presence of a builder craftsman, bored with boxlike houses, who, with assistance from the employees of the granite quarry, would build the house without the necessity for contract bidding. These circumstances led me to seal off my negative opinions about old-fashioned furniture in order to gain a more dispassionate view of the problem.

Acceptance of the furniture as a potentially creative element encouraged an incubation period during which a solution to the problem could be reached. An incubation period during the initial design phase provides opportunities for the unconscious to suggest new relationships and for the conscious imagination to test them. But incubation requires a proper mental climate and the presence of potentially useful past experience that is necessarily different from—yet somehow like—the present situation.

In the designing of the Joyce house, two incubative influences led to my use of the owners' collection as a form determinant. One was my budding interest in the photograph as an object evoking a time set. At that time I was beginning to incorporate photographs into collage painting. The photograph as a recording of events at an instant of time, free of most of the subjective pressures of man-made images, was to become of great importance to me in my work. It soon became clear to me that a piece of furniture, like a photograph, might touch off thoughts and feelings relating to a time set and might inject historical references into a new environmental context. Also the appearance of such an object as a part of an image might increase the degree of recovery of the user's personal experience that has been attached to the object. But at the time I started work on this particular architectural problem, my understanding of these theories had not yet firmly meshed

133

with the design strategies of architecture.

The other influence was a conception about form, the origins of which went back to a design theory I had held earlier. According to this conception, the form of a building might be developed as a changing manifold—a continuous surface that could be formed to respond to specific requirements of usage. In the Joyce house, certain windows that the owners had in their collection were built into this manifold; the length of one side of the octagon plan was partly determined by the fourteen-foot backbar; and the roof of a bedroom warps up to accommodate an exceptionally high bedstead. The finished form, with its protrusions of various sizes and shapes, suggests that it could have accommodated other objects had it been necessary. Before the enlistment of the manifold device, a compact two-story scheme had been decided upon, to restrict foundation and mechanical equipment costs and to afford economical tall interior spaces helpful in absorbing the scale of heavy furniture and large chandeliers.

Mr. Joyce had requested a house that his understanding could "grow into" in ten years, an unusual request that could have inspired various kinds of responses depending upon the architect. His remark, together with the open landscape and the remoteness from other houses, encouraged me in the establishment of the strong exterior-interior contrasts of the house. These contrasts are between the aggressive and the protective and between the closed and the open. As in the Prairie House, the exterior covering is a metaphoric suggestion of the sheltering hide of an animal or the crust of a geode. The juxtaposition, in the same view, of the open transparency of the delicate, crystalline interior with the crustlike, enveloping shelter of the exterior heightens a sense of mystery. Mrs. Joyce was not sure she liked the strange elevation drawings of her house, but she did not want to change the functional arrangement of the plan and was happy to see most of her prized possessions intricately embedded in the scheme. She was also pleased by some of the exterior features that she could recognize—the "steeple," the "mansard," and the octagonal plan. Mr. Joyce said he liked the intentions that were communicated to him by the drawings, and Mrs. Joyce decided to defer to his judgment.

The architect should be concerned about the user's possible incompatibility with form sets that are "aggressive" and "strange." One type of response to this concern is given in the next section, but the Joyce house demonstrates some strategies for keeping a particular image acceptable to the user. First, many form sets that respond directly to the user's experience are integrated into the entire composition of the Joyce house, of which the "aggressive" exterior is only one. Some sets that are familiar to the user are the tall, symmetrical wall forms, curved wall forms that relate to Victorian and rococo furnishings, the octagon plan, the white color, and a bright, clean quality in keeping with the Scandinavian preferences of the user. Moreover, supposedly "unsettling," "aggressive" form sets, if based on deeply harmonized experiences of nature such as the contrasts between the aggressive and the gentle, will awaken chords in most of us that can eventually tune these references to some harmonious concept. The reason for including such references in the first place is to provide contrasts that increase the opportunity for the user to reach a deeper, more complex experience than would be possible with a blander and more stereotyped image.

In an image it is possible to present the beholder with a multitude of cues and impressions all at once. It is difficult, if not impossible, to give a serial account of the accumulation, the overlap, and the many directions of the meanings that one cue will provide for another in the image. However, a listing of some characteristics of the image may indicate the possibilities of multidirectional meaning. The site of the Joyce house is arid, although beautiful, and the fountain at the center of the house offers the sight and sound of water. The center of the house is white, crystalline, and almost completely symmetrical, providing visual cues appropriate to period chandeliers and furniture with gilded trim. In every direction is some glimpse of view either of the granite bluff or of the prairie horizon. Out of sight of the old-fashioned furniture the carport, sheathed completely in shingles, twists into nonparallel forms to harmonize with irregular boulders and to include a "non-Euclidean" form that could allude to the new and unfamiliar in contrast to the familiar geometry of the main house. On the interior as well as the exterior, messages of private and social spaces are combined in the image. The upper level, with its cloister of bedrooms, is juxtaposed with the see-through transparency of the social spaces below.

The center of the house has mild allusions to a sacred place. The sensory cues reinforce one another strongly in this area. The height here is surprising—gentle but soaring. The sculptured stair landings come together in a gesture of touching, as if there is some sort of communion or transaction between them. In the waters of the pool below the landings one sees reflections. One can look past the center of the house to the boulders and plantings beyond.

For all our efforts to analyze the synthetic process in art, we are confronted with mysteries that seem impervious to analysis. And yet our moments of insight goad us to pursue the mysteries, in the hope that patience, detachment, and fresh combinations of ideas will give us further understanding. But while it is often a source of sheer enjoyment and can be very helpful in adding to an understanding of art, analysis remains an end in itself—the processes of rational thought reduced to language. And since art images include integrations of experience that are only imprecisely and elliptically described by language, it is probably futile to pursue analysis with the conscious intention of developing an actual program for the construction of works of art.

# 17 FAMILIAR OBJECTS OF
# USER & DESIGNER

*Historical evidence seems to indicate that the design, use and reten-*
*tion of objects is an ACCUMULATIVE process like learning or*
*growth. The design doctrine of functionalism on the other hand*
*implies that it is a SELECTIVE process, whereby different conditions*
*demand successive and radically different personality orientations.*

Martin Pawley, "The Time House"

Architectural theorists have begun to recognize that individual users need to be able to make their domains their own by imprinting something of themselves on their designed environment. One way for the architect to assist in this process is by incorporating the user's personal objects, which are the physical reminders of his existence, into some meaningful relationship with the design.

Until recently, most design theories have not taken into account that the particular experience of an individual is his context for determining the meaning of an object. In fact, the regard or disregard of the relationships between an object and the psychological experiences it evokes forms a major line of division among design theorists. At one extreme are designers who can see no reason why one object should be more relevant than the next. At the other, are those who feel that a major task for environmental designers is to coordi-nate the sensory cues of selected objects within an appropriate context so that the cues may trigger directed feelings of participation from the users. The coordination of cues requires the selection and control of many different design factors—ranging from the texture of objects to their literary connotations. Throughout this work it is assumed that designers of all kinds need to produce such coordinations.

The coordination of form sets valued by the user seems to me to be an outgrowth of the theory of organic architecture developed by Frank Lloyd Wright, somewhat altered by added emphasis on user experience. Wright's masterpieces display a unity derived in part from the patterns of biological growth. All parts of the design entity are modeled as offshoots of the same seed. This biological analogy, I believe, stands as one of the important ordering generalizations of its time. It is a model of unity based on the testimony of organic growth. As a consequence of this conception of unity, Wright tended to see furniture and ornament as close formal extensions of the forms of the house itself. Chairs, for instance, were often made into geometric shapes that could be found in the plans and elevations of the house itself.

The complex of memories by which human beings establish their identity, however, is not directly analogous to the continuity of biological growth. It seems important to recognize the user's preferences in objects, such as pieces of furniture, in order to establish vivid image gestalts to which he can attach valued experience. This does not mean that the user's furniture should in all cases be incorporated into the design. Rather, the furniture should be considered as a source of sensory cues that are meaningful to the user. Sensory cues of familiar objects may act as keys to unlock feelings and experiences that the user has associated with the object. The notion may be extended to include not just the cues of particular objects, but forms, colors, or arrangement patterns the user has come to prefer—low spaces or high, for example, or protective enclosure or open views.

Wright would have subordinated such predilections to the design of the whole, but they may be treated as individualized design elements. In human creations such as art images, it is possible to achieve a unified construct in which the elements are abstracted from many different experiences in space and time, as the entire history of art testifies. Gothic cathedrals and Wright's architecture are alike coordinations of elements derived from social, religious, artistic, and structural principles that originated in many different times and places. The model of biological growth itself has become one such principle.

I approached the design of the Joyce residence (figs. 55-58) as a problem of devising a unified construct that would consciously allude to the users' objects. The symmetry, the high ceilings, the curved wall shapes, and the color fields of white, green, and granite pink are responses to the users' furniture and dispositions for such contextual settings as a Scandinavian white, bright interior. The octagon plan of the house is also seen as a form historically appropriate for housing a collection of Victorian artifacts.

In the Cunningham house the users' large collection of books and their desire that books be accessible throughout the house resulted in bookshelves built into the balcony rail of some sixty-five feet in length. An alcove, made by the projection of a portion of the balcony into the two-story space, is visible to the entire interior space. The alcove displays books and acts as a symbol of the importance of books in the lives of the users.

The Ward house (figs. 59, 60) has seven levels that meander down a wooded hillside. The owners had become attached to the spatial character of a fragmented, Tudor-style garage-apartment in which they had lived for several years. The apartment was situated in a neighborhood of sumptuous period houses of the 1920s, set in a generous and mature landscape. The architect's first design, which was more symmetrical and had fewer levels in order to lower construction costs, was disapproved by the owners. A house that would necessitate climbing and movement around obstacles had become a valued object for the owners.

Another kind of user object is a proportional set to which a user might have attached meaningful experience during the course of his lifetime. We have already seen that certain proportions in the French residence (figs. 47-49) are a response to the proportions of early Kentucky houses that the users had come to admire. The height of the hallway is a reflection of high-ceilinged early buildings, which often possess an awkwardly high aspect. After discussions with the users I could see it was essential to reconstitute this sense of awkward height in the new house. This height, however, is only one of the important visual gestalts. The low eaves that slope to within four feet of the ground create an image with the horizontal scale bequeathed by Frank Lloyd Wright. The owner (as well as the architect) was interested in Wright's ideas about human scale, and the house provides him with a reference to Wright's work.

Another characteristic of this house is its appearance of being set flat on the ground, without step or transition. This is a characteristic of many older houses in the Bluegrass region; they sometimes look adrift in a sea of clipped grass and white fences. The lack of a modulated accommodation of house to grass is often disquieting, but some Kentuckians are attached to the image. To the users, the "flat on the ground" characteristic had become a valued object. The design solution treated the connection of house to ground in two ways. From the end elevations, which are the more public entrances, the white stucco walls intersect the grass without transition or planting of any kind. The stone walk is held flush with the grass and flows without step into the main space of the central hall. The two broadside elevations are treated differently. Here long low roof lines are themselves close to the ground. The entire intersection of the wall with the ground is edged with soft foliage and ivy, making for an intimate merging of house and land.

When the architect discovers proportional sets that have become meaningful to users and reconstitutes them in new environmental contexts, a link is formed between the experiential resources of the user and his environment. Although a designer can never free himself completely from selections determined by his own personal codes of valued proportion, he can devise strategies to accommodate proportional sets arising out of the design situation. The composition of the Joyce residence was a result of the architect's predilection for low-eave, ground-hugging, human scale combined with the user's admiration for the height that was in keeping with his collection of antique furniture. The reader is again cautioned to envision the process of adjustments as an imaginative construction that alludes to past experience but does not seek to produce a replica of it.

139

Some architects are drawn to systems of proportion such as Le Corbusier's Modulor, in which satisfying perceptual relationships are derived from the Greek golden section and other mathematical ratios. These architects believe that an intrinsic value in certain ratios makes them appropriate for all design situations. But the effectiveness of systems of proportion is drastically reduced by both physical and psychological facts of perception: changes in the angle of view obviously distort the perception of proportions, as do cultural experiences that have programmed us to see only a part of the world about us. Moreover, a system of proportion becomes meaningless unless lived experience of the beholder can be attached to it. The strict use of systems of proportion can become monotonous also, unless rhythm, content, and other factors are considered. The difference between Le Corbusier's work based on his Modulor system and the work of most other architects employing it is Le Corbusier's extraordinary sense of plastic form, metaphor, and drama and his ability to construct imaginative new images of historical archetypes. When we see his work, it is these characteristics that supply the majority of messages to our experience. The harmony of measurements is almost barren of psychic meaning without a vivid sense of the adventures of the actual things that are measured.

As an architect I would treat proportion as a spatial adjustment within a composition. In buildings the adjustment should provide human scale and a unifying sense of purpose and, above all, should express some experiential value for the user. A particular set of proportions may demonstrate an attitude held by a social group. The proportions found in the Gothic cathedral give us an example. The medieval builder was thought to be devoted to mathematical ratios, but we have no firm evidence that such ratios either inspired or regulated his soaring piles of masonry and stained glass; nor can the advances in the technology of masonry from Roman to medieval times explain the new proportional preferences in the later period. The impetus for the Gothic form seems to have been a religious imagination that we can scarcely comprehend—the offspring of a time when man believed he could rise to the contemplation of the divine through the senses. Scholars have superimposed Leonardo's "proportional man" or golden sections onto the facades of these cathedrals with what seem to this writer the most insignificant results.

Conflicts will inevitably exist between the attitudes and predilections of the user and those of the designer. The architect should be conscious both of his pet images and of his preferences for particular proportional sets. It should be with some caution that he imposes them on designs. This suggestion runs counter to common practice. Architects and users alike are accustomed to accepting a parade of formalized images. The formalized image is like an easily recognized trademark to identify an established value system—whether that of Le Corbusier, Wright, Miës, Stone, or

Yamasaki. Whatever the merits or causes of trademark images, they almost always fail to reflect the experiential resources of a particular user or group of users.

The Joyce and French residences illustrate attempts to coordinate user and architect dispositions toward favored objects and images. These houses are described in detail elsewhere; I would allude here to the creature metaphor that is apparent in the Joyce residence but lacking in the French residence. In the Joyce residence, the site and the disposition of the users helped to inspire the ambiguous creature imagery. For the house in the Bluegrass, the users' aversion to neighborhood controversy, their clear image preferences, and the settled local tradition and landscape acted to diminish the use of an overtly mysterious imagery. However, both houses show the architect's disposition for angles and planes, a characteristic that did not seem inconsistent with his interpretation of the users' requirements.

To those who resent the architect's imposition of his own imagery upon the user, I would say that it reflects a tendency never to be entirely overcome, even by the "service only" architects who offer a neutral aesthetic and endeavor to supply only objective, technological knowledge. Even the so-called neutral aesthetic is often coded and bound up in strategies that automatically result in rectangles or other stereotypes of architecture; these also can be considered impositions. However, if a meaningful solution to the major functional and aesthetic demands of the users is provided, the users may become sympathetic toward the architect's imagery and participate in it with their own experience. They may have a tendency to reconcile the unfamiliar, even unpleasant, aspects of images by giving them less attention than the major aspects that are favored and more easily harmonized. The less reconcilable features after a time may actually contribute depth to the images by providing additional contrasts. However, I reiterate the opinion that an architect is obligated to omit images that he knows will irritate the user.

Finally, the user may gradually become aware of meanings in an image that are different from those ascribed by the architect. It turned out to be unnecessary for the Joyces to respond to houses that "look like birds," since they responded to some of the psychological messages of softness, to feelings of a "protective covering," and so forth. The Joyces seem to respond to these messages, as did their relatives from Sweden who visited the house. Their acceptance of these qualities was probably enhanced by their recognition of other visual cues in the image, such as the encompassing "great roof," well known in northern Europe, and the symmetrical, white interior, which is also a familiar feature.

An approach to design that encourages a dialectic between objects of the user and objects of the designer has yet to be seriously developed. The technique of collage, to be given fuller discussion in the final section, is seen as a promising design strategy that can accommodate both types of objects.

141

# 18 USER PARTICIPATION

*In the action of changing and creating an environment the individual confers meaning on the environment.*

Martin Pawley, "The Time House"

Many recent housing projects have proved unsuitable to the social and psychological needs of their users. In response to this problem some architects are attempting to perfect architectural models that will enable the user himself to shape his personal domain. The aim of these architects is to design a physical framework flexible enough to permit the user to express his aesthetic preferences and enter into the physical acts of changing and creating his environment. Martin Pawley, a contemporary English architectural critic and historian of housing, states that most housing built in this century has failed to recognize the need of users to participate in the shaping of their environment.[1]

Designers appear to be the unwitting agents of an authoritarian technocracy that ignores the responsibility for violence done to the human consciousness by its workings. Mortgage companies and the engineering-oriented building industry can be held partly responsible. Public housing agencies are also partly to blame, employing architects trained in behaviorist and bureaucratic strategies and dominated by functionalist theories of design. Such designers have fostered the continuing reproduction of countless housing models that have already proved to be social and aesthetic failures. During the past twenty years, huge housing projects in Saint Louis, Caracas, and London, to locate a few well-publicized examples, have failed, more or less disastrously, to meet the real social and psychological needs of the users, even though the designs embody supposedly high standards of social engineering.

Pawley sees as the basis of the failure the impossibility of reducing the act of dwelling, which is a continuously evolving drama, to a fixed physical form determined from an engineering and behaviorist conception of function. Barren blocks of housing, where the user has little opportunity to impress his personal experience on his fixed dwelling space, are seen as a contributing cause of the anxiety of meaninglessness, which Pawley describes as a well-documented neurosis of our time.

The value of a Levittown, as compared with most housing models, is that the user can accumulate and create as he responds to his house. After planting a garden, adding a room, or creating a new color scheme for the exterior, the occupant may use the visual forms he has established to reclaim the consciousness of his acts long after they are executed. A sense of identity and territory may become intricately woven into the fabric of objects that make up the environment. This physical context confers its limitations and its vistas on its inhabitants and becomes a part of their personality. Pawley sees a verification of these theories in the high status of the single-family estate or house that has a long life and allows a high degree of user modification. One may also point to the more intangible benefits offered by a family home occupied by several successive generations, which offers a basis of stability as well as evidence of experience that is ordered in space and time.

Another manifestation of the user's ties with the environment is the common hostility to redevelopment plans commonly felt by residents of the areas involved. Many are implacably opposed even to the surface appearance of the proposed redevelopment. They organize to preserve and reclaim old and historic buildings. Some choose to live in rehabilitated dwellings of the oldest vintage even though they are perfectly familiar with the modern conveniences they thus forfeit. To these persons, redevelopment may be more destructive than creative. The old environments about to be erased by bulldozers are the physical context of human experience. What replaces them is generally pure form, unrelated to persons or to history. It is Pawley's contention that neither consumer housing nor redevelopment gives adequate opportunity for identification with place or familiar objects.

N. J. Habraken, director of an architectural research organization in the Netherlands, sees the usual housing redevelopment process as not only destroying existing memory-filled environments but also removing individual responsibility for the ordering of environmental space. This happens from the rigid establishment of identical equipment and layout for hundreds of thousands of dwellings at a time. Habraken contends that we must devise a housing system in which the interior arrangement as well as the exterior forms can be altered and updated by the user independently of his neighbors. To obtain necessary population densities, this kind of flexibility must be made possible even in the high-rise dwelling.[2]

While Habraken's program seems logical and even inevitable, if it were to be carried out today, mechanistic design theory and economic forces would unite to produce artless and inhuman housing frameworks of a type already ominously near. Some mobile home parks have begun using high-rise platforms built of concrete; each mobile home is lifted and placed onto a slab in the platform framework. While users have options to change the appearances and make additions to the mobile homes, there is visual monotony in the merely utilitarian superstructure of platforms and in the boxlike geometry of the mobile home and the cheap materials of which it is made.

Other sorts of superstructures of the man-made environment deserve some comment. Just as visible in their effects as the concrete platforms for mobile homes, these superstructures are the form determinants over which the user has little or no control: the mortgage company's requirements, the monotonous street of the subdivision, and the ubiquitous four-by-eight-foot panel of the building industry. Such a superstructure should not be controlled by forces that are largely inimical to the value systems and the psychological needs of the individual. This generality would seem to find easy acceptance where people have been reared on the optimistic premises of self-determination; in my own case, at least, the cheap insurance-financed apartments and the typical housing development touch off feelings of resentment that act as a screen, obliterating whatever virtues of scale, ownership, or territory that such housing may possess.

Yet most people seem to find these current housing products more desirable than anything else available. My negative inferences are made on the basis of the sensory forms produced by the superstructures. As yet, one can only speculate about the ultimate influence of landless, faceless subdivisions and apartment projects on the human consciousness. One fear is that sensory forms will not only be further degraded or sterilized, but that they will actually project a negativity destructive to the consciousness, as may have already occurred in many of the mass housing projects in urban centers.

What ideals do we subscribe to in housing that is to accommodate large numbers of families? The user should be able to create a familiar impression of house and domain within the physical framework of the superstructure. In addition the superstructure should break down into a neighborhood scale so that social contact is facilitated and the image of the neighborhood can be perceived as a unit. The multiples of neighborhoods comprising a community also should have perceptual boundaries and should not be so large or spatially complex that they cannot be perceptually grasped and remembered. The most important goal is that the superstructures should respond to elemental needs of human beings, providing such features as places that inspire people to gather together and contact with nature.

A viable city made up of communities, neighborhoods, and places for work and commerce is easier to talk about than to produce. The results of the planning of recent new towns in England have not been altogether encouraging. We have yet to understand and master the social, economic, and technological forces that determine the form of a city. Yet if these complex forces were understood, we would still need organizational models for the physical design of cities. These models would provide forms able to change without loss of identity; they would display human scale; and they would afford contrast in varying degree, depending on the size of the city. Louis Sullivan's drawing (fig. 72) suggests such a model.

While the design is free and suggests possibilities for growth and change, each part has

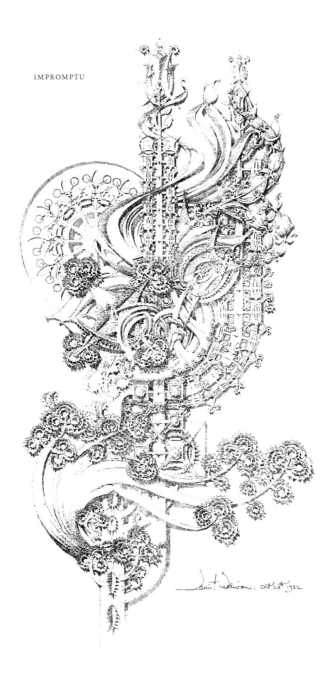

the suggestion of individuality produced with some purpose. Yet each part also seems to reflect the other parts, and this gives the design unity. One can find one's way around in the design by perceptual landmarks of axes, spaces, clusters, and geometric contrasts. One landmark recalls features of another to build an orchestral resonance and a continuity in the mind. This is no mere ornament to grace one of Sullivan's gemlike banks. It is a prophetic speculation on possibilities of human order. Indeed, in this time of concern for the design of cities, one can find in Sullivan's image an ideal city viewed from afar, as from a high-flying plane.

72. Original drawing for *A System of Architectural Ornament,* by Louis Sullivan, 1924
*(Collection of Burnham Library, Art Institute of Chicago)*

# 19 DESIGNER & USER: Custom-Built Houses

*A dwelling is only a dwelling, not when it has a certain form . . . but only and exclusively when people come to live in it. The igloo is as much the dwelling of the Eskimo as the bamboo hut is that of the Javanese. The notion "dwelling" is entirely subjective and is certainly not related to any particular form.*

N. J. Habraken, *Supports*

Experience, according to John Dewey, is "a product of continuous and cumulative interaction of the organic self and the world." David Denton asks us to admit that experience cannot be named and reminds us that we must be content only to describe features of it.[1] In spite of the apparent difficulties, we attempt in this section to demonstrate that the designer can discern significant features of the user's experience and respond to them with the designed forms of architecture. Of particular interest to the designer in his search for significant features of experience are the user's perceptions of, and attitudes about, his previous experience of living in houses; also pertinent are his cultural ties and family relationships, his feelings about nature and the environment, his physiognomy, life-style, and attitudes about human existence. To insure that the design forms that are the designer's responses to features of the user's experience are actually significant to the user, a dialogue between the user and the designer should be established by description, drawings, and models.

An architecture of user participation requires the designer to decide which of the user's experiences are to be tapped. Many of the principles that guide the designer in making these decisions are elaborated throughout this book. Not mentioned elsewhere as an element in the decision-making process is the degree to which attitudes about design are shared by the designer and user. The user increases the likelihood of finding his attitudes shared by his architect when he selects a designer whose executed work he admires. While in theory a designer should succeed in meeting the requirements of habitation for anybody, in practice, conflicting beliefs as well as blindness to the user's experience can lead to failure. I would be apprehensive about designing a house for a Louis Kahn because of the general difficulties of understanding and

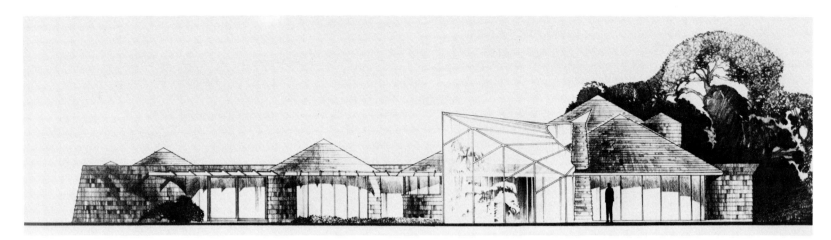

73. Garden elevation of Greene's Mendell house project, 1955

74. Street elevation of Greene's Mendell house project

148

reflecting beliefs that are contradictory to my own. And human experience is so diverse that it is foolish to expect more than partial success in perceiving what has been meaningful to another. However, history reveals architectures and philosophies that have merged once-opposed beliefs and diverse cultural experience. Given sympathy and the time needed to digest sets of diverse experience, a solution derived from apparently contradictory attitudes is possible.

The admission that designers project their beliefs into their work raises a question about an architecture of user participation: how are the beliefs of the designer, as they are manifest in the forms of his work, coordinated with the resources of user experience? It is the assertion here that the design features abstracted from user experience and the forms that embody the designer's notion of significant principles should act together in a dialogue which is a reflection, in a sense, of the user-designer dialogue.

The word *dialogue* suggests a reciprocal relationship founded in sympathy and in a search for meaning. Here it applies equally to the selection of features of user and designer experience and to the manner in which the features are incorporated into the design. In such a dialogue relationship the primary impression of the design image should fit within the understanding and values of the user. This means that the primary image should provide archetypes that speak to the user of similar patternings of things in his own experience. The designer does not treat the archetypes that are suggested by the user as stereotypes or clichés. The ideal nature of the archetype is maintained by the fresh and appropriate expression of other features in the particular design situation. In the examples that follow, some of the possibilities of dialogue between the user and designer will be demonstrated.

The Mendell residence project (figs. 73, 74) was designed for a psychiatrist and his family in 1955. The suburban Houston site was distinguished by many large oaks laced with Spanish moss. The users particularly requested a village appearance. During travels in Europe and Mexico the users had become attached to the appearance of village architecture and particularly wanted this look in the new house. It is necessary to inquire into the values and experiential meanings the user attributes to a particular feature, since such an inquiry can reveal characteristics and relationships that are more significant than the feature itself. In this case it was important to the couple to be able to move among spaces and forms of various scale that would demonstrate perceptually the varied acts of domestic life. Dr. Mendell, in particular, talked of a house that would provide varied spatial experiences, one in which various family activities could be dramatized. He was also interested in avoiding the rectangular rooms of most houses.

The designer who chafes at user requests for a village look in a house as a lapse into the picturesque would do well to inquire into the human need for perceptual models that illustrate the user's conception of a house. The

149

asymmetric growth resulting from the addition of rooms, gables, and other appendages to accommodate new family members and added social uses provides a house archetype in many cultures throughout the world. The symbolic and functional gestalts of these older models can be reconstituted in new contexts, where they can act as a resource for users, helping them to establish meanings derived from their cultural experience.

An understanding of the archetype becomes critical when a designer appropriates a visual model from the past for use in the present. An archetype or ideal type that is used must elicit meanings consistent with the patterning of associations established in previous experience. At the same time, an archetype must express fresh meanings pertinent to the present situation; it must possess individuality as well as appropriate references to a previous type. Degradation of an archetype occurs when a visual form that has been established in experience is applied to a new context unrelated to the earlier patterns of meaning, as when Doric pediments are added to gasoline stations.

In the Mendell house the archetype is established by including important cues that suggest both visual and functional meanings of earlier forms. Figures 73 and 74 show the living area, kitchen, bedrooms, stairs, and storage closets articulated in circular forms with peaked roofs. They are contained by a curved wall that gives privacy from the street and, in the context of clustered circular spaces, provides experiential metaphors of the protective and the maternal. The visual gestalt of the cluster is as much an outgrowth of the functional and operational arrangement of the house as it is a memory trace of the visual appearance of villages. The cluster can be read as a perceptual model of this functional arrangement on the inside as well as on the outside of the house.

The size of the house, budget considerations, and available technologies led to a selection of wood frame and shingles for building materials. The choice of light wood framing and shingles to make an enclosure with plasticity of form was influenced by earlier houses of Richardson and Maybeck, who also appropriated historical "house" gestalts of pitched roofs and bay windows. Another element in the Mendell project that draws support from the earlier American works is romance, here defined as the imaginative transposition of the images and connotations attached to the building styles of other places and other times into the architecture of the here and now. Such a transposition can enrich present experience by associating it with the valued experience of previous time sets. In the present day most transpositions of this type result in merely denotative applications of traditional forms, such as the Tudor fronts on drive-in restaurants. However difficult it may be to formulate a satisfactory role structure serving the interests of the user and an ethical art, the establishment in the new image of time sets that are symbolic of a valued part of the user's experience is an aim of architecture directed to user experience.

A review of the user's remembrances of the houses he has lived in sometimes reveals resources that can be used to provide meaning in his new environment. The project shown in figure 75 was designed for a professor of medicine, his wife, and four young children. The site is a suburban lot by a small lake in Lexington, Kentucky. To the surprise of the architect, both husband and wife presented wallet-size pictures of the houses in which they had grown to adulthood. Dr. O'Neill was born in Ireland and was raised in a very large, symmetrical, nineteenth-century suburban house in Dublin. Sue O'Neill grew up in a very large white clapboard New England house situated amid wide lawns. It was irregularly massed with steep roofs and several porches. Both users had the notion of a generous, many-roomed house with several levels as a background for a ceremonious family life. Their parents' houses and the life-styles associated with these dwellings helped to form their idea of a house as an important expression of one's social, cultural, and professional life.

Any number of solutions exist for the problems of a particular design. The task is to find one solution that satisfies user and designer and falls within an allotted budget and an available building technology. The key idea in this solution was that of stacking the various rooms within a relatively simple single volume that could be read as large, gabled, and many-leveled. The spaces within are distinguished by perceptual and functional differences in roof heights, windows, wall fin-

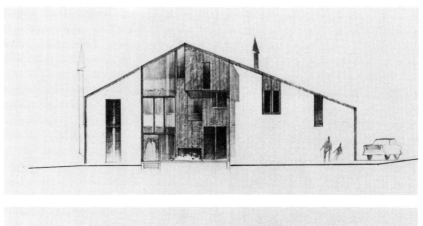

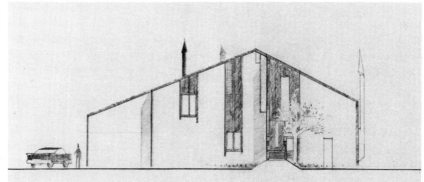

75. Elevation of Greene's O'Neill house, 1967

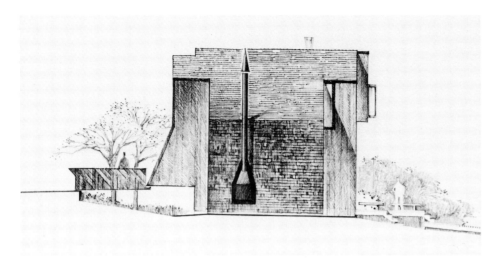

76. Elevation of Greene's O'Neill house

ishes, and built-ins. Windows are sized and placed to give information about the kinds of activities that might occur behind them. The interior exposes the many rooms, overlapping, tiered, and accumulating against a high, three-story open space used for formal dining. The tiered upper floors project into this space and have casement windows opening onto it. Finishes are off-white gypsum board with dark brown wood bandings and trim. Some walls are one-by-twelve-inch diagonal structural wood boards, stained dark brown with vertical rows of fasteners revealed as ornaments. The uppermost volume at the third level is a game room with few windows. It is stained a deep umber and provides a mysterious attic visible from ground level.

Dr. O'Neill, a champion of Irish arts and letters, can respond to the metaphors of medieval street, inn, and great hall, which are among those created by the interior space. Allusions of the exterior to north European pastoral buildings are reinforced by the shingled roof that is carried down the side walls (fig. 76). The absence of overhangs and the asymmetry are faint reminders of early New England wooden houses. The build-up of the many interior volumes contrasts with the single encompassing roof. The sense of many in harmony with one is strong; a spatial dynamic with rhythm, progression, and ascending or descending movement contributes to this sense. House and family contexts suggest various strategies for harmonizing these various kinds of cues.

In 1968 it was difficult to find a contractor

in Lexington, Kentucky, who would build an architect's one-of-a-kind house. Because of ever-increasing costs and the necessity of depending on indifferent, unskilled subcontractors, this house was designed for familiar wood frame construction. Many windows are standard, and cabinets and doors are picked from catalogues.

Space has been regarded by many modern architects as the principal vehicle for transmitting aesthetic value. Frank Lloyd Wright often spoke of the "space within" as the primary reality of architecture. Le Corbusier developed an architectural system which afforded "free space." As a result of the discoveries of these and other spatial innovators of twentieth-century architecture, in the past several decades we have seen a variety of dynamically complex spaces devised. However, many of these most recent expressions of space fail to establish satisfactory bonds of meaning between the users and the elements defining the space. These physical elements tend to be barren of data that have any meaning in the experience of users. They make little or no allusion to appropriate historical forms available to user consciousness, and they make few contrasts in texture, color, and configuration in response to the existential experience of users. Space is reduced to the definition made by bare geometric construct. Many a modern balcony suffers from this architectural malady. In the modest three-story space of the O'Neill house, the play of spatial dynamics, demonstrated in rhythms, accumulations, and overlappings, is combined with allusions to objects and experiences derived from the consciousness of the user.

Shown in figures 45 and 46 is a project for an American family of the seventies in which a house is thought of primarily as a background for acts of experience and as an instrument for shaping their realization. The design aim is to provide resources for the users that could encourage their awareness of their acts on both intellectual and sensual levels. This is a conscious attempt to make the assumptions of existential philosophy—with its drama of choice—contribute to the form of a dwelling.

The site is a wooded farm in central Kentucky. The ground is high, and a clearing falls away to wooded valleys. At the edge of the clearing an ancient farmhouse makes a substantial ruin. Two stone chimneys, timbers twelve inches square, and collapsed roofs are to be made safe and left to posterity. The new house is designed for a couple; one is a city planner, the other is studying veterinary medicine. They are interested in ecology, but above all they are interested in people. The house is to be an experiment with materials, for the sake of conservation, and an attempt at forming a poetic space for human action.

An elongated symmetrical plan was discarded after the users' dispositions toward space became clear. They wanted a house as one large space, a space expressive of a family being together, one space including many. They wanted eye contact between the kitchen and all the public areas of the house. The

153

house is conceived as a series of wooden platforms which make stages, seats, and other usable spaces descending the gently sloping site. The largest platform is in the center of the house. It is a place for something to happen—an encounter, music, a movie, a Christmas tree. This platform is easy to identify as a stage, but it also fades into the sequence of platforms (most Americans need time off for indifference between acts of decision). One flat white wall serves as a movie screen and forms a backdrop to the stage.

Surrounding the center platform on three sides are spaces differentiated in response to requirements of use, specific pieces of furniture, views, and problems of sun control. Each window is different to meet these same requirements. The spaces are outlined with a framework of wooden poles and crossbeams, not unlike the framework of a Japanese farmhouse. Doors and windows can be attached to the poles and crossbars. Pottery and utensils can be hung, alcoves can be formed, weaving can be draped. The pole framework allows the user opportunities to take possession of his house physically and perceptually. The bedrooms have diverse capabilities. One has an outside entrance for a live-in mother-in-law or a workshop. Another can be library or guest room. Another has a platform for children's play. The vintage iron bathtub faces a view of the valley. The tub alcove is a luxurious size, but otherwise the opulence of standard American luxury in plumbing is decisively avoided.

The outer framework of poles is draped with a tent conceived as a background of image resources. Urethane foam is sprayed on mesh to form the tent. Emerging from the foam on the interior are user objects—photographs, mementos, and tools—which have been foamed into the walls and ceilings. Such objects are reminders of the users' experiences and, it is hoped, will make interesting sculptural relief. Additional abstract sculpture and texture will also be attempted with the foam on both interior and exterior. Where the interior spaces might trap heat, the foam would be coated with gypsum plaster as a precaution against fire. The exterior is covered with wood tapestries to protect the foam from decay caused by ultraviolet light. Made of short, salvaged boards, these tapestries are stained off-black and left to weather. The foam tent turns the water and furnishes shelter even before the users and their friends install the wood tapestries. Since the tapestries can be crafted by unskilled labor, the user can assist in determining their design. Small areas of the exterior foam are built up into sculpture and left exposed, where decay is not a problem, and the exposed foam turns rust orange. In the natural setting the orange bits peeking out from the black tapestries will suggest layers and skins, mixing qualities of the natural with those of the technological.

An increasingly popular model of subdivision planning for affluent Americans is the grouping of houses to overlook the greens of a golf course. A golf course provides a permanent green space and a recreational and social facility enjoyed by many Americans. The houses surrounding a private course and club-house are usually expensive. Typically they exemplify ranch, Tudor, colonial, and other assorted styles affirming the taste of the user, each one unrelated in design to the next. The Cunningham residence (figs. 77-79) is located in this kind of setting.

The owners are Dr. Cunningham, an orthodontist, and his wife, the owner and operator of a bookstore. They had become avid golfers and were active members of the country club. Both owners requested a fine house, one that would be comfortable but not cozy. Neither Mrs. Cunningham nor her husband was interested in kitchen or hobby shop domesticity. Mrs. Cunningham had become aware of architectural philosophy through her reading; she was interested in a house that could make an important philosophic statement but did not want a traffic-stopping curiosity. Both owners wanted to avoid upsetting the neighbors.

The Cunninghams' furnishings included bent plywood and Danish blond wood furniture. Scandinavian glassware and Riija rugs from Finland were favorite possessions. Mrs. Cunningham preferred fabrics with natural colors and textures—for her clothes as well as for her furniture. Both her conversation and the objects she chose to have about her disclosed an interest in quality gained by form and proportion, with execution in homely fabrics such as denim before it had become fashionable. She liked the Oklahoma common red brick of the house in which she then lived. The brick was flash-marked with cream-

77. Exterior of Greene's Cunningham house, 1965 *(Julius Shulman)*

155

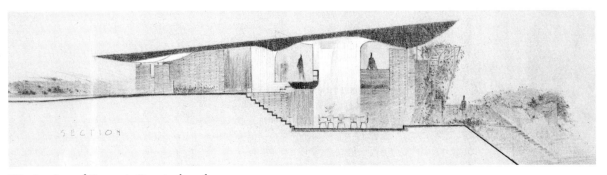

78. Section of Greene's Cunningham house

colored irregularities, providing a feminine quality to what is usually a masculine material. We used the same type of brick in the new house but included vertical rows of dark umber headers to harmonize with the umber wood soffits. Lighting was important. Mrs. Cunningham wanted direct rays of sunlight to penetrate to the heart of the interiors. At night indirect lighting was to soften glare and shadow.

The house was designed for a lot with a fifteen-foot embankment sloping down to the golf course. Viewed from the street side the house presents a visually restrained, low, one-story facade formed by brick walls with few openings. The severe effect is partly the result of designing for privacy and partly a withdrawal from the surrounding colonnades and other examples of architectural heraldry. The visual interest is primarily on the interior where the users can enjoy it.

The roof is a tilted plane. At the street entrance a continuation of the roof descends to confirm human scale and to protect and welcome the users. This roof projection drains

the entire roof into a reflecting pool, with a waterfall effect. The top surface of the roof, covered in brick chips to match the brick walls, is designed for effective waterproofing and for minimal visual interest when viewed from the street. The under surface hovers and soars, differentiating the interior spaces and responding to the rolling greens and prairie horizons. The roof is tilted with an up-and-away gesture that this architect has sometimes found valuable in expressing a sense of human longing and aspiration. The under surface of the roof is made of rough-sawn cedar boards. The deep umber stain grows gradually lighter until it merges with the golden red color of the unfinished cedar boards that are farthest from the source of natural light. This gradation of color acts to lighten the interiors. It also harmonizes with the variety of wood furniture and is in counterpoint with the undulating rhythms of the ceiling forms. The underside of the roof was conceived as the most expressive feature of the house in order that the walls and structural roof might remain of simple construction. It was hoped that the plans would attract local contractors and increase their confidence that they could handle this kind of job. Nonetheless, much of the building is like handcrafted sculpture, requiring a degree of craftsmanship, attention to detail, and careful supervision that under present market conditions is being priced out of the reach of all but the wealthy. Strategies to cope with this situation are developed in the courtyard city example in section 20.

The front entry of the Cunningham house is an eight-foot width of glass, a gesture of openness and welcome in contrast to the privacy of the high brick walls. As soon as one enters, the greens of the golf course are visible beyond the living spaces. These spaces, including dining, living, and kitchen areas, are recessed into the hill. One descends into a protected, enveloping space, and at the same time the roof is seen to lift toward the horizon. The free-standing brick piers and trellises beyond the glass offer a sense of privacy and help to mark off a defined place for habitation. Brick paving starts at the street and flows essentially uninterrupted down the steps, through the living space, past the piers, and down the escarpment to the green. The paving loses its identity as a sidewalk or as a floor confined to a room. It is dramatized as a continuous field upon which occurs a grouping of sculptural events. The piers and the trellises, for instance, happen on this field. The drama between the user and objects in the field is heightened if the field has the characteristics of a stage, or, as here, is a

79. Interior of Greene's Cunningham house *(Julius Shulman)*

157

discernibly unifying layout with appropriate qualifications of texture, placement, and form. The piers and trellises were devised to filter the summer sun through vines. Since this exposure was to the southwest, redwood slat blinds had to be provided as a second line of defense where pictures hung in places exposed to the sun. The functional deficiencies of the trellises are compensated for by the delicacies of shadow that result. The trellises, thought of as sculptures in their own right, suggest an image of sending or receiving information. The suggestion is reinforced by the animate, lifelike aspects of the roof and is probably related to the "looking out at the world" images suggested in figures 13 and 57.

It was Dr. Cunningham's idea to face the escarpment with brick and thus avoid maintenance of a steeply sloping lawn. The resulting brick base or pedestal for the house with its narrow stair adds formality and lessens the sense of approachability from this side. Given the somewhat public location on the golf course, we consider this characteristic to be an asset. The house as viewed from the golf course is meant to be impressive, but it is made so by forms that act together as a harmonious combination of experiential references: a recessed space sheltered by a massive roof, a habitation that fits the land, a responsiveness associated with animate life, and a lifting off that suggests freedom from being bound to the earth.

In a country as large as the United States, possessing such diverse climates, topography, and resources, it is remarkable that there is not more diversity in the styles of subdivision houses. The colonnaded colonials with little-used porches, the gypsum-board chateaux with mansard roofs, the contemporary boxes with flat roofs, and the low-spreading ranch-style houses are everywhere and vary little more than particular models of automobiles. The subdivision house offers the user the prerogative of choice only within the limitations set by the builder, the developer, and the finance company. It is evident that most of these houses present images that have become standardized consumer articles. In the words of an English designer, "The success of a house as a consumer article requires that it can be readily owned, embraced, and understood."[2] One personalizes the subdivision house in much the way that one embellishes a standard automobile—with a choice of options. Bay windows and fireplaces are selected as one would choose white-walled tires or automatic drive.

The economic and social forces that foster standardization have combined with an American penchant for freewheeling manipulation of historical styles to produce the stereotyped images so visible through the land. From the viewpoint of organic architecture as propounded by Frank Lloyd Wright and Louis Sullivan, architects of the European Renaissance had already erred by appropriating Greek and Roman porticos for use in the houses of European nobility. In the late twentieth century an aerospace engineer drives his Porsche into his new colonial carport; the

Greek cornice has made an odd journey from enshrining the gods of Delphi to enshrining the economic and social values of such a twentieth-century American. In subdivision houses the cornice is a contemporary sign of having "made it" and has rather incredibly acquired connotations of coziness. The current prevalence of set-piece colonial or Tudor house images is not really surprising. Americans, according to Gertrude Stein, tend to make imaginative leaps in their thinking. They acquire symbols in one context and use them to make incisive meaning in some new context that is apparently remote from or unrelated to the original one.

In most cases this capacity seems to work more successfully with language than with architecture.[3] Economic and technological constraints, zoning laws, and possibly a more self-conscious attitude toward decision-making in architecture seem to produce more stereotypes than successful archetypal references and sometimes produce some visually bizarre results. An example is the Howard Johnson restaurant. Viewed from the exterior, the image includes a Georgian gestalt of hip roof, cupola, and weather vane. Yet the roofing material is usually plastic tile of a bright orange color. Even before the days of color research for advertising agencies, this hue was recognized as a stimulant to good appetite; it is also highly visible from a passing car. On the interior, the restaurant is like a collage, with glass and chrome modernity mixed with homey light fixtures and wood paneling details that look as if they were

taken from average American subdivision households. The image is a clear example of the pattern that prevails in the majority of American buildings. The layout and technology of these buildings is standard. An image is applied as styling—traditional, modern, or both—to a shell that is largely unrelated to its veneer.

In light of our tendency to treat a building as a shell that can be decorated according to stylistic preferences, the advent of the mobile home has had some interesting consequences. The exterior of the mobile home has proved difficult to decorate in a manner that will provide a time-honored house image, and many people who live in mobile homes have found that they no longer need the psychological comfort provided by the house images of subdivisions.

In 1970 about 33 percent of the new housing units in America were mobile homes.[4] This percentage represents an enormous growth in the use of mobile units and is partly a result of the inflated costs of producing, financing, and maintaining conventional housing models. But there is also evidence that the increase in the number of mobile homes is symptomatic of an erosion of the values of permanence within a mobile population living in the milieu of social and financial independence. Indications are that for an increasing number of purchasers economy is not the major motivation for choosing to live in a mobile home: monthly costs for many mobile homes can exceed the costs of a larger house in a subdivision; furthermore, the mobile

159

home depreciates, while the subdivision house has traditionally increased in value. It would appear that some Americans actually prefer mobile homes to subdivision houses. The "tin can" appearance of mobile homes—anathema to subdivision residents and zoning boards—and their lack of association with traditional house images seem to have fostered a freedom for mobile home owners to engage in personalizing their homes. They can choose to landscape or not; they can park equipment nearby and add rooms on the "front," because they are not concerned with disturbing a house image that has been designed largely for someone else to look at. This breed of home owner seems to have bypassed the need for the status and for the sense of personal identity that comes with a time-honored house image. The interior of the mobile home with one-eighth-inch-thick "wood" paneling and "Spanish Mediterranean" furniture seems to supply traditional image values as well as offering the comforts of home. This is not to say that the owners of mobile homes are known to covet the tin can appearance and slotlike spaces of most current mobile housing, or that they would not respond to more organic images of shelter should such images be made available; rather it is to point out the ease with which many Americans who can afford to do otherwise give up the symbolic values attached to the image of a house.

The apparent flexibility of American attitudes toward house symbols may be considered from several perspectives. From one perspective we recognize the superficiality of symbolic values that can so easily be given up. Many people have but the barest attachment to provincial, colonial, or contemporary styling. On the other hand, the latent flexibility allowing the construction of symbols with imaginative leaps leads one to believe that there may yet be synthesized new models of housing derived from cultural experience and organic ties to nature and at the same time possessing social, economic, and aesthetic relevance to the present. One such housing model will be described in the next section.

# 20 USER DESIGN: The Framework for Public Participation

*For a society of laborers, the world of machines has become a substitute for the real world, even though this pseudo world cannot fulfill the most important task of the human artifice, which is to offer mortals a dwelling place more permanent and more stable than themselves.*

Hannah Arendt, *The Human Condition*

The American preference for living in single-family houses, each surrounded by its own yard, is resulting in a deteriorating visual and social environment. Developers, in building houses to satisfy the desire of Americans to live in the countryside, have all but obliterated the trees and greenspace that were the attraction of the countryside in the first place. In the larger cities one subdivision abuts another with no identifying landmarks in between, giving a sense of sprawl without end. The layout of the single house with side and front yard swallows the land without offering usable space in return.

When we assess the value of the subdivision as a support system for community life, we find that the opportunities for social contact in subdivisions are few. Rarely are there community places or patterns of activity that could bring people together. There are no bicycle paths, pedestrian walks, corner stores, ponds, or copses. In addition, we have found

that the costs of roads, utilities, and services required to connect and maintain the low population densities of subdivisions have risen enormously. The costs of home construction and financing are also approaching prohibitive levels. Unplanned and unhappy consequences of our housing habits seem inevitable in the coming decade.

Yet the subdivision house, which the Levitts have spread successfully even to France, offers opportunities for the user that are hard to dismiss. The user can act upon his domain by choosing accessories and adding appendages. The automobile and camper can be kept at the doorstep. However, because of spiraling costs and increasing transience, many people are becoming less enamored with the permanence associated with land and home ownership. They want to spend less time and money on maintenance, and they resent high property taxes. They want security against vandalism when they leave their homes on

161

80. Greene's courtyard city project, 1971

more frequent vacations, and many want recreational and social facilities integrated with housing. As a consequence, many Americans are moving into apartment buildings and condominiums that satisfy these requirements. And yet, despite the goal of added social contact, it may be that the exodus to apartments lessens the users' sense of community responsibility.

We need new housing models that alleviate the burden imposed by the present machinery of housing finance. The new models should also facilitate the development of socially and politically viable communities. We must reckon with the users' desire for automobiles—a desire which for the present it seems necessary to accept—without crushing the neighborhood with concrete roads. We must be aware of the transience of present-day populations at the same time that we recognize the need to reconstitute neighborhoods and admit diverse life-styles. We must acknowledge the basic need many people have of contact with ground and garden and of participation in acts of modifying and personalizing their domains. Some of these needs cannot be adequately satisfied in apartments and cluster housing.

Preliminary design studies for an alternative to the American subdivision appear in figures 80-82. The design studies address current housing realities such as the economic necessity of mass-production methods and of a more efficient utilization of land and finance. They also attempt to provide a community design that will stimulate social contacts. The

162

recognition of user prerogatives in shaping personal space is an underlying principle for the studies, which aim at the creation of place, continuity, and quality in an environment that also allows for change and transience.[1]

The courtyard is taken as the unit of change. A courtyard eighty feet deep and thirty-five to fifty feet wide is seen as a space with a variety of potential uses, including housing. It is large enough for the user to have a vegetable garden, a swimming pool, or an addition to his house. The courtyard walls are conceived as a permanent framework into which prefabricated housing units may be placed. The housing units themselves would be subject to choice and modification by the user. As improved models appear, the units could be replaced. The permanent walls, the public open spaces, the roads and utilities, and perhaps even the land of the courtyards could be financed over the long-term life of the project, say seventy-five years. The housing units could be financed over much shorter terms. The user might lease his courtyard for tenures of occupancy. In any case the yearly cost of housing for the user would be reduced by the financing of the long-lived framework separately from the short-lived housing unit.

The images to be projected by the wall framework include those of mass, texture, scale, and form not obtainable from the prefabricated units themselves. Certain walls are thickened to provide habitable space or to accommodate community facilities, such as laundries, small stores, or recreation rooms.

One purpose of the thickened wall spaces is to provide the user with a space of nonmanufactured character. These thick-walled, cloistered spaces provide contrasts with the lightweight factory-built housing units. The textures, geometry, and space of the permanent thick-walled units would be different from the prefabricated thin-walled housing. Spaces within the same house that possess different arrangements and appearances would suggest varied possibilities for human uses.

Materials, colors, textures, and shapes of the wall framework could respond to the local situation: landforms, local building technologies, valued local architecture, and climate could all influence the result. Rhythms and a prominent play of light and shadow are general design objectives of the framework. Places are provided for users to impress their own designs on the walls of their personal space. Wide-ranging sculptural allusions are built into the framework, and, in fact, the walls are thought of as sculptures that accommodate housing, mitigating the monotony of the manufactured. The artful design of openings, gates, and gazebos both creates privacy and encourages social contact. Seating, planters, storage spaces, fireplaces, and other features are built into the walls to encourage user modification. The wall framework extending through the neighborhood would create an image of unity while affording the user real privacy within his own courtyard. This privacy would probably encourage more personal expression than the current subdivision model.

163

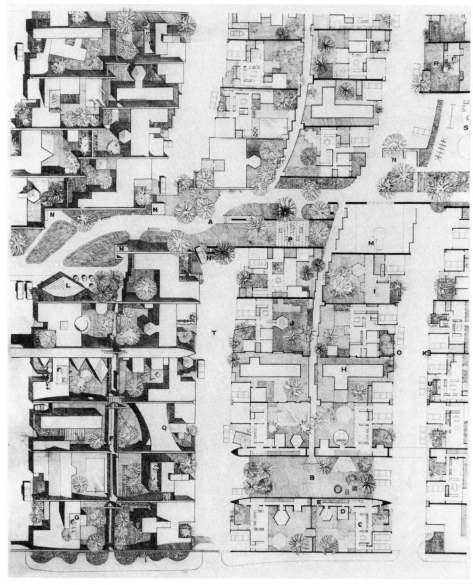

81. Partial plan of Greene's courtyard city project

A  Community greenspace, a five-minute walk from end to end, provides pedestrian path to school, shops, services, and recreation.

B  Neighborhood greenspace serves about twenty housing units; it promotes social contact and a sense of place within the neighborhood.

C  Prefabricated housing unit has components twelve and fourteen feet wide to allow highway transport.

D  Prefabricated module.

E  Thick wall unit, field made, provides cloistered space for retreat and privacy.

F  Pedestrian passage provides buffer between lots but permits social contact. Fences, storage units, gates, and landscaping may be controlled by the user to adjust the degree of privacy.

G  Roof deck gives access to breeze and sun but is protected by adjoining second-story spaces.

H  Industrialized housing unit or mobile housing unit.

I  Elevated court house, suitable for office or studio, leaves ground level free.

J  Two-story module projects above courtyard to catch breeze and to permit view.

K  Trash storage.

L  Snack shop.

M  Paved surface can be used for half-court basketball and other public activities.

N  Gazebo provides a meeting place between each motor court and pedestrian greenspace.

O  Exterior screen walls are made of perforated masonry units or wood fencing; the degree of privacy may be controlled by the user.

P  Picnic area.

Q  Catenary roof. Unusual forms can be accommodated within the framework without undue imposition on the neighborhood.

R  Roof planting is practical on concrete flat plate construction.

S  Community tot lot gives larger space with more play opportunities than provided by the neighborhood lot.

T  Motor court is 200 or 350 feet long with turn-around at end. The visual impact is established by walls arched over the street, screen walls, entrance aprons, gates, carports, the neighborhood greenspace, and the major greenspace at the street's end. The motor court is surfaced with gravel or pavers suitable for people as well as cars.

U  Pedestrian landing and place of contact. Curb-height pedestrian landing is large enough for planting but does not demand it. Kitchen and breakfast areas permit visual contact with the street. Shutters afford the user varying degrees of privacy.

V  Space between adjoining lots allows social contact, although gates give privacy from either side.

The ordinary subdivision bombards us with the sight of man-made objects that demonstrate anything but human care. Metal vents clutter roofs. Concrete sidewalks, porches, and curbs are minimal and crudely formed. Plastic shutters which never close decorate double-hung windows which rarely open. In the courtyard models the walls, street textures, bollards, and fences are designed to allow people to care and to encourage their latent capacities to care. The wall features are attempts to contain the ticky-tack.

But the underlying idea of the wall framework, as likely to be missed or devalued by the critic as by the layman, is the provision of a set of forms that alludes both to architecture and to nature on a scale that is larger than the individual house. The walls would provide allusions to natural landforms and to the valued memories of the architecture and activities of a place. The image desired is that of forms both gracefully controlled and at the same time casual and unspecific enough to suggest to the inhabitants convenient possibilities for the use and arrangement of their individual domains. Many of the individualist prerogatives inherent in the American housing tradition of house and yard can be exercised within the wall features.

The illustrations here show only two of many possible expressions of courtyard frameworks. The project shown in figures 80 and 81 is designed for the southwestern region of the United States. Allusions to mesas, to indigenous Spanish and Indian architectures, and to the rising and falling landscape are incorporated in the walls. The wall features would be permanent constructions of sprayed concrete on urethane foam armatures. Except for precast gates, openings, and inserts for fireplaces and built-ins, the walls rely on field executions by skilled artisans working with sculptor-architects. It does not seem possible or desirable to rely on an entirely factory-made environment. This proposal mixes the handmade, large-scale walls with the standardized factory-made unit. The form is a collage that could incorporate more or fewer visual contrasts depending on location and market situations. A high-rent retirement village, for example, might have less contrast than student housing at a large university.

Modern architectural theory has too long ignored or maligned the intellectual and emotional value of allusions, or the incorporation into architecture of specific objects that have become meaningful to various social groups. The use of objects to stimulate recollections of shared experience is discussed elsewhere in this work. The courtyard walls are opportunities to incorporate into architecture allusions to specific local historical events. The Mayan hut on the nunnery at Uxmal and the simulated rope and piling details of certain fish and chips franchise restaurants are alike in containing such allusions. That the franchise image is visually debased and manipulated to commercial rather than social and artistic ends is not the point. Men need the visual resources of allusion to participate in their cultural stores.

In a courtyard design for Lexington, Ken-

165

82. Larry Gream's courtyard city project

tucky (fig. 82), the sloping metal roofs, brick walls, and occasional tall chimneys are features common in early houses of the town. But the layout of courtyards, superwalls, and streets at once provides them with a new functional expression—one of the ingredients required to transform the visual data of sloping metal roof, for example, from stereotype into archetype.

These speculations on courtyards leave questions unanswered. What are feasible ways of coordinating the users' choice of housing modules with a permanent wall framework? What kind of visual controls would be required? The planning concept suggests that people with varied incomes and life-styles could form a neighborhood, and in theory mobile homes could be introduced within the framework. It is hard to imagine the private sector of the housing business experimenting with new social and economic patterns. And while the government has noticed that social and economic stratification in housing is a contributing cause of social and political ills, it is hard to gain bureaucratic support for new ideas. However, it is my belief that the courtyard framework, which is almost as old as civilization, can be adapted as one valid model for American needs. The well-designed courtyard, as a refuge from a hectic institutional and commercial world, could prove a valued image. Such a framework produces user flexibility within substantial urban forms that could celebrate aesthetic, social, and cultural values beyond the immediate demands of shelter.

166

Our emphasis throughout this book has been on the satisfaction of the needs of the users of architecture. An additional benefit of the kind of housing envisioned in the courtyard design is the effect it could have on those who actually build it. In a day when most workers seem to feel that their labor leaves no distinct mark on the world, the opportunity for using craftsmanship in the construction of the sculptural wall framework could give meaning to a kind of work that too often is repetitive and dedicated to the production of structures that are both standardized and short-lived.[2] While for most people there is more to life than work, dissatisfaction with this part of life is apparently a growing problem and one government and industry may soon have to address.

One of the satisfying images of human settlement is that of the village enclaves, three to six in a vista, scattered through the rolling farm lands of southern France, the steep foothills of Switzerland, or the hills of northern Italy. These settlements appear to be scaled to the numbers of people that once were required to tend the lands that surround them. The image is beautiful, but the way of life that created it has passed. Yet we can draw some conclusions from the satisfaction we feel when contemplating the image.

First, we are able to perceive a community as a visual entity with connotations of physical and social unity. We are able also to see the physical forms of man-made communities that cooperate with contours and features of the land. Contact between man and the landscape is nearly everywhere available and with this accessibility to a salubrious nature comes an unspoken sense of freedom. Here one might come to engage in some spontaneous participatory act with nature, free of the constraints of a man-made setting.

These observations helped determine the design objectives for the cluster of courtyard housing frameworks shown in figure 83. The area marked by diagonal stripes is a typical subdivision in the rolling plateau that is the topography of Lexington, Kentucky. Six frameworks of two hundred houses each are situated on the highest ground. Between the frameworks is open space in a flowing patchwork retaining the pattern of alternate development and open space that characterized Lexington before the uncontrolled expansion of the past two decades. The lowlands along the small streams are developed as pathways for pedestrians, bicycles, and horses. One small stream offers a greenbelt two and a half miles in length. This feature establishes a natural boundary between the cluster community and whatever lies beyond.

Children can walk to school using pathways that are overpassed by highways to eliminate crossings. Within the greenspace the cluster housing, apartments, and high-rise towers provide a variety of housing types and increase the overall density to six housing units per acre. This density is an improvement over the typical subdivision sprawl (which averages three or four units per acre) but, unlike the subdivision, still leaves broad swatches of

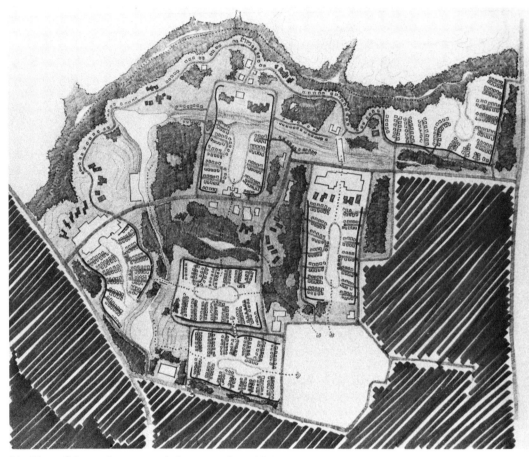

83. Plan of Greene's courtyard cluster project, 1971

open space. The courtyard walls relate to this open space by following the slopes of the land, giving an image, at least, of community in close fit with land. Shops and services are placed at the junctures of courtyard frameworks and highway. Through traffic from outside the development is intentionally discouraged by the design of stops and turns in the highway.

Most highways that lead into our cities are lined with fast-food franchise restaurants and service stations. McHarg calls these strip developments "the quintessence of vulgarity bedecked to give the maximum visibility to the least of our accomplishments" and says that they are the most visible testament to the American mercantile creed.[3] These charges are justified, but the economic, social, and psychological forces that produce the strip probably cannot be wished away just yet. Most of us drive through a strip on our way to work; most of us use the fast food and other services that the strip provides.

While many Americans see the strip as visual pollution, this is not the only way it offends. Based on a model of unlimited access like that of Main Street in horse and buggy days, the strip produces dangerous driving conditions at a time when millions of new cars are poured onto the highways in a single year. But there is little use in bemoaning the ugliness and hazards of the strip or in lauding, as the alternative, the amenities provided for pedestrians by malls and other models of shopping and commercial centers. Frequently

168

we want fast service with the automobile at our right hand. The illustrations in figure 84 are for a strip development that assumes drive-ins are conveniences that serve current American life-styles. The design is an attempt to solve some of the problems that are caused by strip development.

The strip is placed along a highway that connects the suburban residential community with nearby business areas. It is given a service road that restricts traffic to the users. A greenbelt surrounds the strip and affords a buffer—a graceful natural screen that enables the nonuser to pass the strip without being forced to deal with it visually.

The layout of franchises forms a single arc a third of a mile in length. The arc forms a perceptually understandable and functionally simple organization that allows the greenbelt to be close to all parts of the strip. It is possible for the user to do his banking and dry cleaning here and pick up food, liquor, and sundries without leaving his car. The strip could include fried chicken and hamburger franchises, quick-service grocery stores, automotive service, a motel, a motor home hostel, and other drive-in services.

Today the architecture of the strip is largely an architecture of signs. The interior spaces of franchises are often low and cramped to save on air-conditioning and construction costs. The signs, however, are large and highly visible. Some franchise designs integrate the sign with the building enclosure. Other franchises strive for a building "in good taste"; this is apparently the aim of the man-

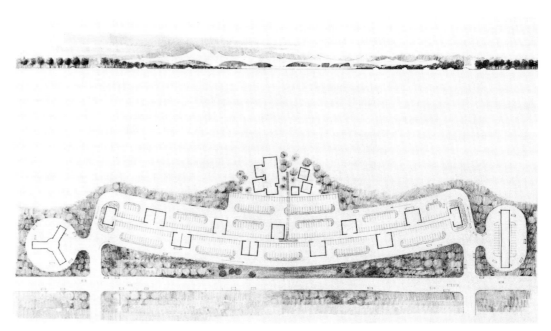

84. Elevation and plan of Greene's franchise development project, 1971

sard roof and warm-toned brick of the later McDonald's models. The strip in America can be seen as a kind of dream world of images rendered in plastic, or a romance of allusions—the bringing of the far near to be set adrift in a sea of parking lots. Overall the effect is more alienating than festive because the buildings lack human scale, the allusions are usually superficial, the buildings are cheap and careless, and the user feels that he is being processed along with the hamburger.

To turn to the appearance of the strip we are proposing, figure 84 shows one solution to the problem of attracting customers without spoiling the scenery. Here the parking lots and

169

franchises are covered with a series of fabric membrane structures supported by a mast system—structures similar to those developed by Frei Otto and others, using membranes with translucent surfaces of great beauty. Up to now these tentlike structures have been used mainly to cover exhibitions and recreational facilities such as tennis courts or stadium seats. Here they cover both the franchise and the car and provide shelter from sun and rain. The sides of the structure are open, and overhead gaps permit the free flow of air. From the highway, perhaps for miles in each direction, the membrane appears to lift out of the greenbelt providing a landmark that is graceful, yet contextually appropriate for the circuslike aspects of the strip. The mélange of independent and often gaudy strip enterprises can be envisioned as a sort of circus and market combined. The membrane tents offer the opportunity not only to make a circus image, but to create mathematically beautiful shapes that would be seen to advantage from a moving car. Lights could be projected onto the translucent parts of the membrane causing a soft glow. The tents could be colored and shaped to be as gaudy or as pristine as might be suggested by a particular site or program.

As for the architecture of the individual franchises, it could be left as it is in the present model with each franchise designed as a distinct trademark, or the buildings could become simple glassed enclosures that would no longer clamor for attention. In this case the franchise sign could be elaborate, but the tents would provide the primary visual inter-est. The user would become aware of which franchises were located on the strip by direct acquaintance and by logos placed on well-designed markers on the approaches to the strip.

To the user and merchant who assert that placement of franchise and sign directly on the highway is required to generate maximum trade, I would say that the current practice of allowing unlimited access constitutes a hazard both to the user and to the nonuser and may actually discourage trade. In addition, the visual pollution of the signs, wires, and vents of a typical strip should not continue as the dominant form-determinant of our cities.

The greenbelt and tents would require greater expenditures than are usual for strip development. The cost of the greenbelt could be defrayed equitably by the owner, developer, and the user community. Depending on the particular site, the greenbelt might be partially paid for by commercial recreation such as miniature golf and driving ranges, but in general it would best be developed for landscape values. We have reached the point that the urban environment is in decay because we cannot break the pattern of developing land with no other goal than maximum profit. Current estimates place the cost of a suitable tent at two to four dollars per square foot. A franchise owner would pay about six thousand dollars a year, since available membranes last only six or seven years. However, savings resulting from a simpler building and reduced need for air-conditioning would partly offset the cost of the tent. Again we have to realize that improvements to the physical environment will entail expenditures over and above the cost of mere facilities to do business.

Viewed from the traditional perspectives of architecture, the design of a typical drive-in business presents us with a crisis in symbolic authenticity. With a mocked-up Nantucket shanty for fish and chips or an Italian arcade made of quarter-inch plywood for a supermarket, the viewer is confronted not only with inconsequential and merely denotative allusions to Nantucket or Italy but with careless and incongruous construction that affects the force of the allusions as well. But in a curious way a positive concept for images in architecture may be latent in the highway Medusa of the franchise strip. It is ironic that the automobile, which has led to the proliferation of cheap mercantile buildings strung out along traffic arteries, also leads to an architecture in which symbolic content is physically separated from the building, appearing instead in the lavish, expressive sign that marks it. This concept could become increasingly useful if the design of road signs should be developed into an art.

In treating the symbolic function of architecture it is helpful to compare the usage of the past with current practice. The column, capital, and architrave of the ancient Mediterranean cultures, for instance, evolved into a complex set of forms to which various significances could be attached. The capitals of columns represented such objects as sacred plants, human heads, hair, or animals. The ancients even appropriated such objects stabilized in architecture to use as mnemonic devices, as Frances Yates tells us.[4] The practice appears similar to recent techniques developed by psychologists to prolong the retention of concepts by associating verbal constructs with three-dimensional objects.

While we no longer use architecture for mnemonic purposes, we do need design strategies that allow us the flexibility to refer to the various types of meanings that are embedded in the building or associated with its use. We also need strategies that allow arresting visual gestures to be expressed in the design, because such gestures are among the most important means of stabilizing, recovering, and expressing human thought. To this goal, modern architects have often taken a negative attitude. In an effort to purge architecture of historical styles and ornaments which had lost their meaning, rationalist modern architects dismissed the role of architecture as a carrier of allusion. An alternative concept of ornament, largely misconstrued or dismissed as a survival from an earlier century, may be found in the prophetic architecture of Louis Sullivan. Sullivan thought of ornament as an expression that could fill out the character or the spiritual intention of a space or a building in ways not accomplished by the main lines and masses of the building. Like the Greeks of antiquity, he used the juncture of capital and beam as a node for intense expression. In his work a unique blend of geometric and botanical forms, the origins of

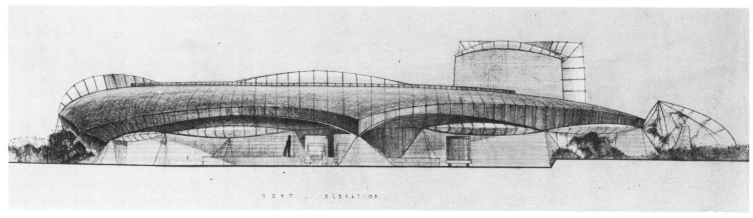

85. Greene's post office project, 1951

which can be traced all the way back to the *Book of Kells*, seemed to aim at rendering an image of organic process with lifelike growth, energy, and continuity.

A disarming example of ornamental allusion to specific life acts is to be seen in the urban panorama of drab warehouses, plants, and offices where, in the sixties, super-sized paintings began to cover entire buildings. These supergraphics seem to be intended to brighten a dull environment and to identify the acts of those who work in the building. They serve as examples of an ornamentation for architecture in which the ornament is not integral with the building. Integral ornament has been a presupposition of Sullivan and the organic school; however, in freeing ornament from the construction of the enclosed space, more techniques of expression are available.

The student project by the author for a post office (fig. 85) shows, at the right end of the drawing, a sculptural element attached to the main enclosure. The interior space of the post office is made by a roof form sheathed in copper and by a sloping wall sheathed in limestone. The sculptural element is thought of as a gesture of ornament in the tradition of Sullivan. The mass and lines of the building are extended into a purely expressive element composed of stainless steel wires and flat bars and a stone and glass pier set amid water and plants. Cost economy, which will be an important point in this discussion of freeing ornament from the physical enclosure, was never an issue in this design. (The building would probably cost nearly as much as an Air Force jet bomber.) But the notion of freeing ornament from the mass of the building seemed to me a concept with great promise.

Today a designer faced with tight budgets,

inflated costs, declining craftsmanship, and the structural problems of waterproofing unusual forms may find himself in a nearly hopeless situation when he proposes a design based on established principles of modern architecture. The expression of program, materials, structure, and the latest technology are, by and large, costly practices in America. The organic positions of integral ornament, integral site relationship, and metaphoric form are, as a rule, also costly.

The concept of ornament freed from the building mass would make practical an architecture that provides symbolic content and expresses the realities of the way its enclosed spaces are made. The combination of a directly functional and economic space enclosure with a physically detached symbolic form would enable the architect to avoid unduly difficult problems of construction. This type of combined form would be subject to a breadth of treatment expressing, often with humor, root meanings of associated words as well as more transitory associations with the building and its use. The two-part concept lends itself to collage techniques and admits allusions that would probably be excluded from the permanence of the space enclosure itself. The neon signs of Las Vegas and Times Square are possibly the closest existing parallels; but I can envision expressions more wholesome, humorous, and heroic than these, if the sign contractors of the future could be staffed with artists and philosophers of human experience, and if their clients could be responsive to similar values.

Many of our high-rise office and apartment buildings do not resemble structures to be occupied by human beings. Viewed from the exterior, they are like sealed containers that offer little evidence of human activity within. Their facades suggest cages or they are blank expanses whose patterns lack signs of human control, intervention, or scale. Many a beholder has transmitted their monotonous messages to his own soul.

Prevailing attitudes toward aesthetics, economics, and technology account for the appearance of the typical high-rise. The rule of symmetry fosters the use of glass walls on south as well as north exposures; so we must overwhelm the sun with mechanical cold. The investor calls for maximum short-term remuneration; design proposals that fail to meet this criterion are abandoned. Some aestheticians go so far as to view the monotonous repetition of the facades of these buildings as inevitable consequences of mass production and a technological era. They interpret the buildings as expressions of natural laws to which there are no rational alternatives.

Besides presenting disturbing images, high-rise buildings promise functional problems. Human wants and uses change within the life span of a building. The owner needs a building that can be inexpensively adapted to changing uses. The user needs a building that gives him freedom to arrange his personal space. An architecture that is directed to existential and cultural communication must answer these needs. A proposal for a high-rise prototype that responds to the requirements

of change and to other functional and psychological needs of the user is illustrated in figures 86 and 87. One design objective is a layout of space that can be adapted to housing, commercial offices, or professional suites. To this aim the building is formed by alternating small spaces (situated in structural towers about twelve feet square) with large spaces (open bays twenty feet wide and up to forty feet deep). The towers carry the mechanical services and are large enough to provide support spaces for offices or, in residential applications, kitchens and baths. The interior walls of the towers are designed for access to mechanical chases and may be overlaid with materials that fit the needs of the user. The exterior of the towers can be made with materials that are appropriate to the site and to neighboring buildings. Important image values of the towers are the nichelike spaces they provide for human use. One "enters into" or "acts upon" the primary perceptual form of the building. The modest width of the tower suggests a space scaled to human size. At street level the towers alternate with glass bays to provide natural entrances and recesses for shop windows.

The towers are highly visible as three-dimensional elements that extend beyond one floor to another, and a sense of dwelling among a cluster of towers is the result. The user occupies a space that may be perceived as being related to a larger whole rather than being cut off from any visual contact with the total three-dimensional structure, as is the pattern in most high-rise buildings.

174          86. Elevation of Greene's high-rise project, 1969

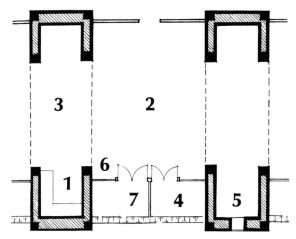

87. Plan of Greene's high-rise project

1   Tower and niche.

2   Open bay with ceiling height of 9 feet 6 inches affords more light to interior.

3   Ceiling is dropped to 7 feet to contain mechanical equipment.

4   Floors or balconies can project according to building program.

5   Towers can be pierced with openings.

6   Glass wall can be 9 feet 6 inches in height at exterior.

7   Translucent vertical sunscreen divides balcony.

The practical problem of screening or receiving the sun is solved in a functional and visually interesting manner. The user can have contact with the outside by means of balconies designed to provide a sense of security appropriate to the height of the building. The balcony allows the user to keep plants and to make his own additions of enclosure, from wind screen to full-fledged sun porch. Balconies, railings, and sun controls are made of identical twelve-inch-deep metal space frames that are open lattices. Used as a railing, four feet high, the space frame provides a transparent structure of snowflake intricacy, which would provide an unusual sense of security because of its depth and numerous members. Used as a floor structure for the balcony, the space frame supports a translucent panel deck made of epoxy. The translucent epoxy panel of three-quarter-inch thickness would diffuse light to the space below. Used as sun control on southern exposures, the space frame affords complex shadows. Additional baffles can be attached to obtain the desired degree of sun control.

Part of the design aim is that the building components should not require exotic technology but should be responsive to local construction techniques and materials. To this end the system is one of small spans and small members organized so that the building can be constructed with either a steel or a concrete frame, to be clad or filled in with masonry, metal, glass, or concrete.

Buildings can be viewed as statements of transition, because they project meanings derived from previous times into new situations with new technological and economic conditions, social patterns, and aesthetic interests. Miës van der Rohe's famous apartment towers

175

on Lake Shore Drive in Chicago can be seen in this light. Miës expressed modern steel and glass technology in a structural cage revealed as the visible form of the building. He presupposed the values of symmetry and uniformity, values derived from a classical past, in producing an image based on modern technology. Miës's solution was to assemble mass-produced elements of modern materials into pristine forms that were designed to reduce visual tensions and to represent a rational expression of structure.

Accommodation to other evidences of design ideals in transition is a proper goal for apartment buildings. A visit to the home furnishings department of a large dry goods store reveals the wide range of traditional and modern styles in current demand. The high-rise framework in figures 86 and 87 is intended to be compatible with a broad range of user preferences in furnishings and in the arrangement of space. The niches, brick walls, perforated railings, and high ceilings are capable of reasonable harmony with either traditional or modern furnishings. Thus the user is given latitude in expressing his own design ideals as carried by the objects with which he surrounds himself. The framework is designed to avoid the visually demanding angles and built-in furniture of Frank Lloyd Wright's Price Tower as well as the austere grids of Miës's buildings, which make the appearance of most user furniture seem an intrusion. In another accommodation to the fact that design ideals are in transition, the building framework of narrow masonry-clad towers,

glassed bays, and visually intricate balconies allows for analogies with the materials and smaller scale elements of earlier urban architecture. These cues from the earlier buildings add a familiar dimension to the large structure. However, the user is encouraged to move beyond the reference frames of older architecture. The tower images appear as soaring solids laced together with glass and metal. The balconies and cantilevered forms at the top of the building make mild allusions to growth and branching, providing metaphors of trees and a sense of purposeful culmination.

Public buildings are usually presented to their users as accomplished facts, by fiat of government and corporations. The physical character of the architecture is often that of an unalterable package with little or no possibility for the user to impress his actions on the building in any constructive way. Occasionally institutions, private or public, have employed architects of remarkable skills to interpret user needs, and some recent designs, particularly of educational facilities, have responded to needs more individual than the general ones of the building's future physical expansion. The users have contributed both to the program and to the form of the building. It is important that the public user be able to participate in acts of shaping his environment. In spite of difficulties in devising and putting into action practical strategies to this end, the current interest on the part of some architects and institutions can be taken as a hopeful sign for the future.

# 21 CARTESIAN INFLUENCES

*The mind in apprehending also experiences sensations which, properly speaking, are qualities of the mind alone. The sensations are projected by the mind so as to clothe appropriate bodies in external nature. Thus the bodies are perceived as with qualities which in reality do not belong to them, qualities which in fact are purely the offspring of the mind. Thus nature gets credit which should in truth be reserved for ourselves; the rose for its scent; the nightingale for its song; and the sun for his radiance. The poets are entirely mistaken. They should address their lyrics to themselves, and should turn them into odes of self congratulations on the excellency of the human mind. Nature is a dull affair, soundless, scentless, colorless, merely the hurrying of material, endlessly, meaninglessly.*

Alfred North Whitehead, *Science and the Modern World*

In this book my principal concern has been to describe an approach to architecture that is very little exemplified in current practice. One can survey the modern architecture of major cities without once finding an example of what I have described as an organic approach to images. Many buildings are not designed by architects, and the images of these are usually a response to utility and popular taste. But even those buildings designed by architects generally contain images that are a response to a tradition of thought inconsistent with the organic approach. In the next three sections I shall discuss this tradition and its manifestations in a variety of design trends.

Man does not have to use modern technology to make buildings look mechanical and like simplified illustrations of geometric formulas; yet the images of many modern buildings seem to be drawn more from the appearance of machines and from the configurations of solid geometry than from any other source. It is my conviction that the tradition of European thought, along with the increasing prominence of machines in our lives, has led to this kind of architectural image.

The tradition of European thought to which I refer may be called the Cartesian tradition. It is not appropriate here to attempt a general appraisal of the influence of this tradition on later thought or on aesthetics in general. It will be sufficient to select certain of its principles with particular implications for architecture and to show to what extent they still seem to be the ruling assumptions of many architects and how their influence appears in certain recent trends in art.

The tradition began with Descartes and was continued by Locke and Hume. While there are significant differences in the thought of these great figures, certain ideas of Descartes underlie assumptions of the two later philosophers. The Sensationalist attitude toward perception they held is given brilliant analytic treatment by Alfred North Whitehead in *Science and the Modern World* (London: Cambridge University Press, 1932), pp. 64-70 and in *Process and Reality* (New York: Macmillan Co., 1929), pp. 214-54.

Inheriting from Greek philosophy the assumption that an object (such as a stone) consists of a substance with inhering qualities (such as shape, gray color, or dampness), Descartes gave new definition to the notion of substance and a new subjective bias to the conception of the inhering qualities. Some qualities were conceived as essential attributes, so that apart from them, the object would not be itself; other qualities were changeable. Both essential attributes and changeable qualities were held by Descartes to "require nothing but themselves in order to exist."

The notion of "independent existence" had also been fostered by the Greeks but received impetus in the seventeenth century by becoming a presupposition of mathematical and scientific formulations. Descartes, in framing a theory of perception that would reflect the rigor of seventeenth-century mathematics, considered the essential attributes of sub-stances to be their most apparently definite and constant features, those features amenable to mathematical treatment, namely "figure, magnitude, and motion." The expression of these attributes for the Cartesian tradition culminated in Newton's laws of motion. Locke, influenced by Newton's laws, added mass to the list of essential attributes.

Independent existence also enters into Descartes's concept of changeable qualities. In contrast to the essential attributes, which were always present in a substance, qualities such as hardness, sound, smell, and color were not always present. For instance, the sound made when a bell is struck is soon dissipated. Thus sound was classed as an accidental (or changeable) quality inhering in the bell. The particular sound of a bell or the particular shade of gray in a stone was conceived as a universal (an entity not dependent on any other entity) apprehended by the mind as it reflects the private sensations of the beholder. To be sure, Descartes admitted the existence of stimuli for sound in the bell, but he believed that the conscious experience of the stimuli "clothed" the bell with the bulk of its sensory output. This separation of the sensory output of the bell from its so-called essential attributes led to the belief that the message of an object's sense data is in a sense an arbitrary property of the mind, as compared to that object's unchanging essential attributes. Descartes's belief that the private conscious experience provided the primary data for thought was, according to Whitehead, "the greatest philosophical discovery since the age of Plato and Aristotle."[1] But Descartes embraced the notion of "independent existence," and that led to the disconnection of the meaning of the color in the stone or of the sound in the bell from other situations in the world in which these particulars are implicated. Descartes also assumed that current forms of speech were complete expressions of conscious experiences. And thus the foundation was laid for an attitude that confines the meaning attributed to sensory experience to certain "rational" ideas introduced at the end of the cognitive process. This attitude discounts the unconscious gradient of experience and the reconstruction of dismantled stored experience that takes place in the initial stages of cognition. The attitude enforces the precedence given to the so-called essential attributes as described by "rational" thought. This set of ideas fostered both the mechanistic bias and the tendency to treat concepts as if they belonged to a self-sufficient conscious mind and not to the wider environment provided by nature.

We cannot blame Descartes for not taking modern psychology and theories of perception into account; but his belief that color, for instance, is a property dependent on the mind's private ideas and not thoroughly intrinsic to the object has had important effects on architecture. Neoclassic architects often executed their buildings in white, ignoring the color of natural surroundings, adjoining buildings, and materials of which the building was to be made.[2] White suited the neoclassic image of an ideal that was pure and supposedly free of the contingencies suggested by color. The use of color for its expression of the nature of materials or for its range of effects on bodily feelings has characteristically been restricted in the classical academic tradition. Similar restrictions on color were inherited by the early modern movement of the International Style.

The Cartesian assumption that essential attributes such as figure "needed nothing but themselves in order to exist" led to another important consequence for architecture. Geometric shape was abstracted from objects and thought of as existing independent of them. But instead of being trivialized, certain ideal shapes were actually exalted. The notion was, of course, familiar to the Greeks, some of whom held that ideal forms (for instance, the geometric constructs of Euclid) existed independent of nature and were ideal types that man should try to achieve in his works. Architects still endow Euclidean cubes and their sections with virtues that are out of proportion to the scientific status of these forms as revealed by mathematics and physical science, which in the last hundred years have investigated the forms of non-Euclidean geometry. A belief that ideal forms exist independent of nature led to a belief that such forms are inevitable and that human beings must seek and accept them. The works of recent European masters often appear to express this belief. Le Corbusier's Ville Radieuse, a symmetrical gridiron city that included repeated towers of Euclidean form, suggests an ideal type, as does the inevitable rectangle of Miës.

179

The Cartesian reliance on the verbalization of conscious ideas about supposedly independent substances, to the exclusion of other ways of knowing, formed a background against which the "rational" expressions of cognition, logic, and structure could be taken as the primary fact of nature itself. The direct testimony of nature, which shows that the growth of organisms requires a continuous process of related transformations and that all things in the world are interdependent and in an ecological relationship, was not seen as relevant to scientific thought. The development of modern biology and other life sciences has forced a reaction against the Cartesian way of looking at the world as an array of independent substances. Habits of thought, however, are not easily changed in their entirety. The Cartesian influence is still apparent in modern attitudes and procedures.

The Cartesian separation of essential attributes has come to foster the visual neutrality favored by many modern designers. Since emotional experience is derived from the private world of sensation, it is subjective. It cannot meet the requirement of being measured in a perfectly definite manner. Intrusions into design that seem emotional, spontaneous, or incongruous do not meet the Cartesian requirements of rational thought; the same could be said of any experiential metaphor or any subjective projection of an emotion. But machines are considered products of rational forces, and designers have begun to feel secure in using forms based on their appearance and on models of their functions.

The rational mind believes that it can construct functional models based on the operational and the instrumental and that it can coordinate them with the requirements of physical structure and the "engineering" of social behavior. These beliefs have been transformed into design goals by the rationalist progressives. The visual forms that express these aims are thought to be universals, free of subjectivity. I contend that these forms are not neutral at all, but merely the result of viewing the design problem through the Cartesian filters of ideal types and of giving precedence to verbalized rationalizations about the structural relationships of objects over their existential and phenomenal properties. The so-called Cartesian attitude accounts for the fact that the complex metaphoric processes at the base of knowledge have been overlooked. These processes occur in response to an awareness of objects that is screened out by the prerequisite of a clear, mechanist formulation of the functions and operations of separate physical entities.

The building shown in figures 88 and 89 is an expression of the Cartesian attitude. What counts in this building is largely the rationale agreed upon by the makers of the image and their audience. The rationale produces strategies for accepting exposed heating units, boxlike spaces, and prefabricated panels as valued perceptual forms. The strategies obviate the necessity for rhythm and keep at bay any feelings of boredom or dullness that may arise because of the minimal sense stimulus of the building.

88. Model of Walker and Hodgetts's rental building project
*(Reprinted from* Progressive Architecture, *copyright 1969, Reinhold Publishing Corporation)*

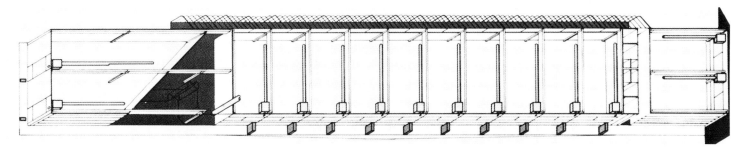

89. Drawing of Walker and Hodgetts's rental building project
*(Reprinted from* Progressive Architecture, *copyright 1969, Reinhold Publishing Corporation)*

One test of an art image has always been its ability to stir feeling once the social and intellectual issues that shaped it have suffered erosion. Except for the sheer novelty of the unfamiliar, Indians from ancient Uxmal would probably walk right past the building as a valuable aesthetic experience. The social group responsible for the example may know nothing of the Indians at Uxmal, but it is unlikely that they could walk past a fragment of that city without realizing it was a valuable aesthetic experience.

The belief that the material world is governed by irrevocable, codifiable laws (not, of course, original to Descartes), appeared in his time in scientific guise. It is assumed that every occurrence can be correlated with its antecedents in a perfectly definite manner, according to knowable general principles. The belief in irrevocable, codifiable laws that govern all events implies a belief in a "remorseless and indifferent" world, as Whitehead says, with a vision of fate urging an accident to its inevitable issue. It is a vision still possessed by science, and it has been a part of Western culture at least since the time of the Greek tragedians. Descartes reflects this view: man can think about the universe, but he is powerless to change it, for it is a relentless mechanism operating by unchanging laws. The influence of the belief appears today in the general acceptance of the uncontrolled rush to the employment of machines to replace the skills of men; to many the process seems as natural and as inevitable as a tidal wave.

One other mark of the school of thought we are labeling Cartesian is a disregard of specific context. For architects this means that the actual character of site and region does not enter, explicitly, into the subject matter of concern. The character of individuals as experiencing, psychological beings has no bearing on design, and the preferences of the particular ethnic or other social groups that are to be the users of the architecture are ignored.

Many twentieth-century architects have been influenced by one or more of the Cartesian presuppositions. The eclectic classicists McKim, Mead, and White, for instance, subscribed to specific Greek and Renaissance prototypes as proper sources of imagery. The classical school of thought that had attributed perfection to Euclidean forms now attributed the same perfection to the architectural forms of Greek temples. Unimpeachable values were assumed to exist in these specific forms of classical antiquity. Further improvement of the forms was considered impossible. The modern rationalists Miës van der Rohe and Gropius reacted against historical eclecticism but directed themselves to images of function, technology, and social reform and favored a Cartesian order based on Euclidean geometry, symmetry, and uniformity.

Cartesian influences also appear both in the everyday architecture of the large corporation and in the radical projections of such representatives of the avant-garde as the Archigram (fig. 90). Despite many outward differences, both kinds of buildings are intended to merge building technologies and solutions to social problems in images that express primarily the operational aspects of these concerns. A mark of both these design directions is a preference for "machinelike" images. Space is often enclosed as if by a container derived from industrial processing. Circulation systems for people are often made to resemble the circulation systems for conveying materials in an industrial process.

The designers of the building shown in figure 91 explain that it "expresses a system of enclosure that is related to the performance requirements of other physical entities such as automobiles, the body, or airplanes."[3] The designers compare the permeable, flexible, sensitive skin of the human body with the impermeable, rigid, glass skin of the building. Their analogy is apparently based on purely functional similarities between the two ele-

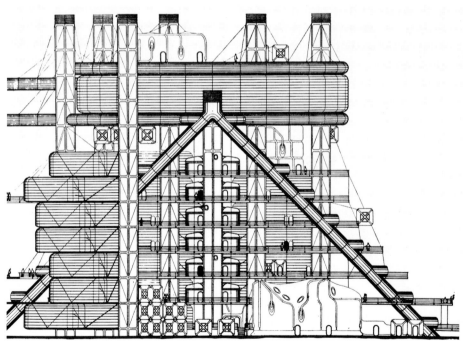

90.  Archigram Plug-in-University Node, 1965, by Peter Cook

183

ments. The validity of even this part of the analogy can be questioned, but my main point is to call attention to the emphasis that the designers place upon operational and functional requirements and to their very language, in which machines and their workings provide the dominant symbols. It is true that current advocates of architectural reform continually stress *process* and desire to demonstrate it in images, but they confine their interest largely to a process of technological procedure and operational principles. Most organic processes—such as the life experiences of man and the rich metaphoric activity of the mind—continue to be tacitly subordinated.

Of course this account is oversimplified, and it must be admitted that the bulk of the man-made environment is produced by a commercialism that is several times removed from the direct influence of Cartesian filters. But it does seem clear that the influence of the Cartesian filters inherited from the Western tradition is still the dominant force in architecture today. The result is the projection of architecture into images that reveal great stress on operational principles and structural technological systems, while using form sets derived from classical biases toward uniformity and symmetry, and, more recently, from machines themselves.

91. Daniel, Mann, Johnson's office building, 1970 *(Wayne Thom)*

# 22 CHAOS, CHANCE, & AUTOMATISM

*I write about what is in front of my senses at the moment of writing.*
*I do not presume to impose "story" or "plot" or continuity.*

William Burroughs

The Cartesian influence appears in many forms in the current world of art and architecture. Advocacy of temporary, disposable architecture as the logical outcome of the search for maximum flexibility and freedom from historical encumbrance, trust in the eventual omnipotence of computers in the design process, and acceptance of industrial containers as models for human habitations—all these are attitudes that fit under the Cartesian umbrella. Another attitude that seems to have connections with Cartesianism is the simultaneous distrust of unconscious guidance and of introspective design ideas.

The mechanistic view of the world is among the particular philosophical bases of the movement which discounts both the depth of the unconscious and the worth of consciousness. The latter position would seem to contradict the value Cartesianism places on consciousness, but actually this recent trend of discounting the rational is a mechanistic, about-face reaction to the apparent failure of rationality to deal with the proliferating and conflicting issues of the contemporary world.

Before this trend arose, mechanism had fathered (as now it continues to foster) the automatic and behaviorist approaches to individual and social acts. It has provided the model for our technology, which is currently developing in uncontrolled, unmastered growth. People's lives seem swept along by the sheer momentum of technology. It is as if the glut of technological objects is produced by a relentless universe rather than by men who have the power to alter the production of these objects. In the face of this situation, introspection seems futile. Hence, the turn to sensory appearances rather than causality and to the surface and the sheer presence of objects rather than the human sentiment attached to them.

Distrust of the power of the subconscious, the inheritance of a mechanistic cosmology and of the current reaction to it, and the paralyzing insecurity introduced by positivist attempts to establish rigorous limits for word meanings have caused many artists to feel they are reflecting the "real world" when they portray a chaotic randomness and the

185

domination of man by the machine.[1] The artists of this group have a pronounced interest in the chance circumstance as a source of imagery. According to the sensationalists' theories, one object representing randomness should be as good as the next. In the actual practice of many of these artists, however, social agreement, fashion, direction of interest, and other forces conspire to narrow the range of permissible objects in the agglomerations of incidents in the artistic "happenings" of the last decade, for instance, and among the "banal or ordinary objects" of pop art. In their enthusiasm for the chance circumstance, the artists circumscribe a range of objects which allows them to dramatize chance as the lack of coordination between events. Objects are chosen for their disparity and unrelatedness. For viewers who are not attuned to the values tacitly or explicitly attached to the random, the unexpected soon becomes monotonously predictable. The normal role of the consciousness seems to be thwarted when its field is restricted to isolated sense impressions. The consciousness has evolved as our primary instrument for organizing our experience and seems to insist upon going on with its work.

A further disadvantage of media happenings is that they rely on unrepeated events. During the transfer of attention from the "Now and Here" of an image to the "Then and There" of its referents in stored experience, the flux of circumstance may influence the process of transfer. Qualifications may be introduced by the mood of the percipient, by details in the external environment, or by quirks in the particular patterns of thought called into play by unconsciously perceived details in the image itself. The transfer experience is of a transitory nature and is susceptible to dissipation, blockages, and wrong turns. One value of a stationary image is that the viewer is free to associate with it or dissociate from it at will. The stationary image may be experienced at different times with different gradients of attention. The artists who use new media need to recognize and preserve these values, which are inherent in stationary and recurring images.

This criticism of the use of the chance circumstance in images should not be interpreted as a dismissal of randomness when it is found within a work that presents a coherent view. Countless artists have successfully integrated the chance circumstance into their work, where it provides contrast to the professed aim or formula of the image. Thus chance in an image can be a reference to a world that is wider than the aim or formula. It is the use of chance to present chaos that I question.

In the creation or interpretation of an image, consciousness fosters an awareness of coherence, but many artists have confused consciousness with the sheer perception that is its raw material. Whenever images seem to issue from concern for details, the consideration of alternatives, or unhurried planning, they are held suspect as anachronistic by these artists, who are reacting against the mode of creative process that traditionally involves a time-consuming dialogue between conscious ideas and unconscious guidance and the struggle for adequate expression. The strength of this reaction against the carefully designed, well thought out, and thoroughly worked-over image seems at least a partial explanation for the recognition given recent architectural projects that minimize careful visual detail. Judging by these projects the image should be an operational model, no more artistic than a diagram of a gasoline engine—its functional parts adroitly brought together without the appearance of either subjective or consciously aesthetic intercession in the placement of the parts. This kind of image is presented by the building in figures 88 and 89, in which modules of rental space and air compressors are mechanically repeated and juxtaposed against a glassed-in circulation corridor.

Another reason for the demise of care and detail is the prospect of early obsolescence and replacement. The fact that building forms are to change rapidly in the future is seen as eliminating the need for the traditional worked-over piece of "permanent" architecture. It is felt also that the pace of modern life does not encourage people to participate in the visual intricacies of a traditional architecture. The emphasis of this outlook is on the functional, operational relationship between the human being and the building. Little attempt is made to elicit the psychological feedback that is the normal manifestation of human sensitiveness. Human scale, human activities as dramatic acts, and allusions to

nature are given minimal attention. I recognize that a blunt pragmatism aimed at economic efficiency is an important cause of much of the technological imperative, but an attitude that would dismiss human sensitiveness is also unmistakably present.

The use of the mass-produced, interchangeable parts presupposed by the obsolescence theory, however, could be considered as an exciting and practical development if genuinely flexible and qualitatively acceptable parts should become available. Nor am I denying the interest and beauty of many machines; the hardware of many manufacturing processes has value as a source of imagery. My objection is to the assemblage of commercially expedient parts to project an image illustrating only the bare operational or functional aspects of a facility, as when, under the pretext of a scientific determinism, objects such as nondescript casings of air compressors, which offer minimal possibilities for human empathy, are selected as primary ornaments for a building.

The design for the low-cost commercial building shown in figures 88 and 89 received the first honor award in a national publication on architecture. The building could be anywhere. This is a virtue in the eyes of those who harbor Cartesian codes of universality, as is the fact that the building could be used for any purpose: school, garage, factory, or retail store. The jury, in making the award, saw the solution as a foreshadowing of an architectural environment to come. This building is organized and cannot be called random in the

187

same way media "happenings" are; but the concern for presenting the building merely as a manufactured object has led to the celebration of certain random operational aspects of the building, such as this year's model of the air conditioning compressor, suggesting that these aspects are felt to be appropriate stimuli for the human consciousness. The final expression is, I think, an image of mechanical and anti-human determinism. The image of the machine seems to have usurped the place of images of human intervention in the world.

# 23    THE POP IMAGE

*It is fairly clear that pop offers no new "internal" developments for painting; its formal and technical language is not original, it is a thematic art, hence it raises questions of attitude and value orientation.*

Edmund Burke Feldman, *Art as Image and Idea*

*Modern man, body without soul, tossed about by hostile forces, was ultimately nothing else but what he appeared from outside.*

Nathalie Sarraute, *L'ère du soupçon*

The abstraction of selected aspects of an object for consideration is a method indispensable to human thought. The Cartesian attitude suggests that the mind can endow any selection of these aspects with a self-sufficient meaning that is impervious to the intrusion of other aspects of the object. In this respect, the "pop" movement of the sixties, which glorifies the outward appearance of ordinary objects as art, is pertinent to this discussion.

The pop image shows a fascination with objects taken from popular culture. The graphics of billboards and images of hamburgers, movie stars, and motorcycles are often magnified to huge scale as if to rescue them from our routine acceptance. These images also feature mechanical and constant repetition, as does the advertising world in which the objects are often found. The technique of the artist is usually kept anonymous and impersonal, as if to avoid any expression of ego-involvement or subjectivity.

Artists since the time of Duchamp have realized that an ordinary object can be rescued for use as an art object merely by presenting it as one or, more reliably, by changing its frame of reference, as with Picasso's bicycle seat and handlebars made into a bull's head. The pop school salvages not the bicycle wheels and hatracks of Duchamp's "readymades" (which often do suggest meanings beyond the customary utilitarian role of the objects employed), but comic strips and catsup bottles—objects with minimal capability of self-transcendence. Most important, the manner of presentation is purposefully deadpan, as if to stifle the introduction of any frame of reference beyond the object itself. The rebelliousness against sacrosanct objects and attitudes in fine art is evident, but this particular rebellion was successfully carried out by artists early in the century.

The pop school in architecture, like the pop school in art, seems to enjoy the self-conscious use of the banal object. Perhaps, once more, this is in reaction to the difficulties posed by introspection and the use of unconscious guidance. For the proponents of pop architecture, the character of the kind of commercial strip found in Las Vegas is accepted as a fact of life and taken at face value. The strip, with its supposedly direct response to the problem of getting automobiles from the airport and to the bars, hotels, gasoline stations, and wedding chapels of the city, is accepted as a model possessing virtues that are both operational and visual. The strip is seen as more fitting to the motorized and fragmented American urban life than is the European square favored by so many university-trained architects. In denying the appropriateness of the European square for Americans, I rather agree with the pop advocates, although the banality and the functional difficulties of the strip hardly seem the best alternative. But traffic hazards and all, the strip is accepted as an object not to be interfered with, in much the same spirit of deadpan objectivity as the catsup bottle is.

The strip is admired by pop artists for its random juxtapositions of the large and the small. These artists abstract fragments of neon and billboard for use in new designs to increase visual complexity and to promote milieu consciousness. But although pop archi

tecture uses milieu fragments in new buildings, they tend to be confined within plans and spaces derived from Euclidean squares and their diagonals, circles, and semicircles—forms probably approved more by architects of the modern classical tradition than by a popular audience. The visual effects derived from juxtaposed scales, colors, and graphics, so evident in the actual untidiness of Main Street, U.S.A., tend to be applied to the favored Euclidean forms without evidence of causal relationships.

The use by pop architects of the ugliest commercial metal windows available seems intended to force our acknowledgment of a new canon for appreciation of the window as an art object. In 1915 Bernard Maybeck used industrial steel windows in a Christian Science church at Berkley, California, but the windows became absorbed in his transcending statement in a way that the pop school does not entirely encourage. In Maybeck's church the industrial window unit appears as a sign of the commonplace within a design that is warm, intimate, dignified, and humanly mysterious. Maybeck also massed the standard windows and subdivided their panes so that their formal properties make an image that visually transcends the utilitarian connotation of the window. This is quite different from presenting the beholder with a banal object and relying solely on an intellectual attitude to generate appreciation of the object.

Another early example of the incorporation of objects from the everyday milieu into buildings is Bruce Goff's use of the circular

Butler grain bin for housing. In several house projects in Kansas and Oklahoma, Goff employed the standard corrugated metal bin that is much in evidence throughout the midwestern farm belt. The familiar bins are insulated and either painted various colors or used in their factory galvanized finish. Figure 92 shows a design with unifying fascia, a carport, windows, and corncrib-turned-screened porch—all signs of human scale and habitation. The pop attitude of recognizing design values in everyday objects is already evident in Goff's work, but as in the case of the industrial windows in Maybeck's church, Goff's appropriation of an everyday object results in a transformation. The harmony made by juxtaposing concepts of housing grain and housing people in the Goff composition, is, in a way, similar to the VW bus-Superman collage. Surprising consistencies may be found.

We recognize other precedents for correlations between the forms made by artists and nonart forms developed from exigencies of the times. Gertrude Stein and her painter friends of 1914 noticed that the camouflaging designs painted on trucks en route to the front were very much like the work of certain painters of that period. According to Stein, everyone is of one's own time, but it is the artist who recognizes and records the perceptual and conceptual composition of a time while it is being lived. Everybody else who actually lives within the composition is too busy or too indifferent to be conscious of it. When forced to be cognizant of the artist's

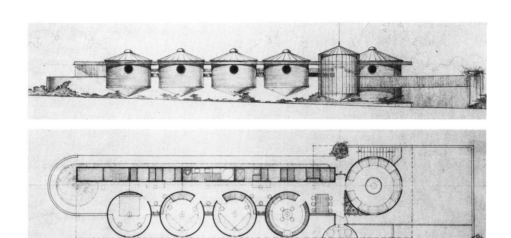

92. Residence project by Bruce Goff, 1955

composition, he tends to think in terms of the art of a previous time.[1] Pop architects of today tend to keep one foot planted in the previous time dominated by Euclidean forms and Cartesian strategies while trying to live consciously in the pulsating neon of the strip and Main Street world of juxtaposed perceptual effects.

Neon and billboards provide sensory excitement and a feeling of immediacy, but unwanted facts associated with the myriads of gas stations and billboards that inspire the pop school are dismissed in true Cartesian fashion. The juxtaposition of perceptual effects, as of the wedding chapel neon heart and plastic cherub seen against a giant Texaco sign, is accepted without a quiver of reaction

191

to the life and meaning of the objects. All we do is sit back and enjoy the purely visual tensions produced by the light, color, and line. The crux of my criticism of the pop school is that the experiences associated with the history of the object cannot be forever held at bay by special attitudes that focus attention on qualities of shape or on some other attribute of the object. The knowledge of what the object is—toilet seat, soup can, or ugly window unit—may not be dismissed. The dadaists made the point that any given aspect of an object may transcend the object's usual or functional context. We now see objects more clearly because of this discovery. But out of the multitudes of objects in the world, why must we be pelted with the meanest sort?

Banality in itself is not the real flaw. Some banalities are peculiar to neon and the strip, and others are peculiar to a stone head of a Mayan maize god. Some perceptual cues evoke richer, more complex harmonies of experience than others. The maize god communicates states of being and feeling that allow us to harmonize its banalities on deeper levels. Ultimately objects cannot escape from their adventures in the world. Concepts of how they arose, what they are, and what they lead to enter into the feelings they produce. Consequently, the artist must acknowledge this aspect of the human response to objects as he selects the objects and controls the frames of reference in which they are seen.

It is my contention that the enlarged hamburger or ugly window of the pop image represents one more phase of the sensationalist tradition that depends upon the Cartesian separation of an object from the totality of feelings about that object. Feelings are automatically set off by our coded experience of the character of an object. That feelings are not supposed to interfere by intruding upon the conception of the object as an inviolable piece of the universe, subject only to unchanging laws of mechanism, is the subconscious directive of the seventeenth century. According to this tradition, the mind is a spectator; faced with an object external to itself, the mind perceives and reasons but does not interfere.[2]

The influence of the pop objectives may be seen in the architecture of the Archigram group and such designers as Robert Venturi. My criticism is not directed against all the stated objectives or executed work of these architects. Their use of historical puns and their criticism of inappropriately monumental and heroic buildings are evidence of an attitude that supports neither a compulsive discarding of every reference to the past nor slavish imitation of it; in their development of complexity and ambiguity by allowing the expression of construction techniques and program requirements to intrude into the image, these architects pursue a worthy goal; and the inclusion of fragments of the everyday world to increase user participation is a technique with enormous possibilities. It is the choice of objects to be placed in images and the sensationalist attitude toward them that we criticize.

# 24 ORGANIC ATTITUDES

*The process itself is the actuality.*

Alfred North Whitehead, *Dialogues*

It is as evident to the biologist with his microscope as to the sociologist with his statistical studies that the world can be viewed as a system of interdependent organisms. Every organism is influenced by the earlier stages from which it has developed. Every organism is influenced also by the present situation of which it is a part. These are basic assumptions of the organic attitude that have been developed during the past century by philosophers, scientists, and artists.

Among the considerations of the organic attitude is the effect of these influences from the past and present upon thoughts, memories, and unconscious mental activity—in short, upon the psychological life. An objective for those holding the organic view is the achievement of an organic wholeness in the psychological life of individuals and groups. An architectural approach that strives toward that goal by attempting to create symbols of significant personal experience can find support in the works of various theorists. Bergson conceived of the self as an entity existing through time. He regarded the personality as expressing the unitary character of an organic whole. He believed that the events and feelings of one's life, made accessible by involuntary acts of memory or intuition (such as appropriate symbols can stimulate), revealed the most significant evidence of the self. And William James stressed a reality based on the individual's perceptions, beliefs, and actions that arise out of present situations and local and specific contexts. For James, as for Bergson, the activities of the individual consciousness replaced the nomothetic abstractions of universal law regarded by traditional European philosophy as the central determinants of meaning.

Turning from organic theories of personality to a consideration of the methods of attaining truly organic composition, we note the view of Henry James, who characterized the novel as a "living thing, all one and continuous . . . where in each of the parts there is something of each of the other parts." James saw the novel springing from a "germ," a seemingly small, often inauspicious event that starts a growth and elaboration in symbiotic relation to some wider intention in the mind of the novelist. The idea of a "germ" is paralleled in the theories of Louis Sullivan, who conceived of a "seed germ" as the initial impulse of a design that is maintained throughout its many stages of development.[1]

193

In this book images that include diverse orders of things have been described as attempts to express meaning in a way that more closely resembles an organic process of cognition. The influence of Sullivan on these attempts has been pointed out in our discussion of the synthesis of images. However, we can also point to the applicability of the views of Henry James in that a seemingly inauspicious element in a problem situation, as, for instance, old-fashioned furniture in the case of the Joyce house, may be used as a point of departure for the elaboration of major themes in the design. The use of such elements in the design of a building offers the user specific landmarks of lived experience. A landmark to which lived experience has been attached suggests a specific consciousness-to-object relationship of the type familiar to readers of William James.

The furniture in the Joyce house was incorporated into the image by the technique of collage. While a number of design strategies can be used in an organic approach to the design of images, I believe collage offers one of the most promising alternatives to the methods that rely on uniformity, mechanism, and the notion of independent existence.[2] The importance of collage lies in its expression of diverse themes within a single work. Among the themes of the Joyce house, as we have seen, are an exterior form manifest as a crust or sheltering roof whose elements include references to the aggressive as well as the protective; a crystalline, white interior; nineteenth-century windows set in forms with anthropomorphic references; a "teepee" screened porch; and a massive granite base, which "presents" the artifacts of the user and sets the place apart visually from the boulders of the site.

The ordering device of collage can be used to present, in a diverse collection of objects, contrasting references to time and history, to the experience of the body, and to the expressions of character that are embodied in the objects themselves. Symbols of valued personal experience can be included in the collage, and organic relationships between diverse objects can be expressed.

Perhaps the most significant recent architectural expression of time, history, and bodily experience is Ronchamp. Collage is usually designed to include found objects; the towers, walls, and roof of Ronchamp can be considered as created objects that are composed in the spirit of collage. The four sides of the building are surprisingly different from one another. Each side expresses a unique set of functional and symbolic intentions. Figure 1 shows the tower, great roof, and thick wall of the entrance side. A backdrop for outdoor services is seen in the adjoining side. Figure 93 shows the grouping of towers, which abound in anthropomorphic, religious, and regional architectural references. The remaining side displays relatively anonymous windows and is expressive of subordinate spaces within the chapel.

At about the time of the design of Ronchamp, Le Corbusier's aphorism that architecture is a series of plastic events became well known. Le Corbusier's phrase would seem to allow for the architectural expression of the diversity of character of different kinds of activities. For instance, outdoor services are provided for by the vivid expression of a chancel by the overhanging roof, two pulpits, the curved freestanding element at the right, and the vertical end of the great wall on the left. But Le Corbusier's choice of words also implies that he learned much from his career-long pursuit of painting and sculpture. The assemblage of diverse cues noted in our discussion of the Picasso paintings (figs. 8, 28) is also apparent in Ronchamp. The juxtapositions of cubism were well known to Le Corbusier, as they were to other architects of his period. But unlike most of his contemporaries, whose responses were usually limited to repeating the formal geometric structures of cubism, Le Corbusier used cubist modes of organization to assemble contrasting references to culture, history, and the bodily life in what he so aptly described as a series of plastic events. The relationship of this method to collage should be evident.

Among the explanations given for the genesis of cubism was the necessity, in describing the reality of an object, of presenting more than one of its spatial and connotative perspectives in juxtaposition. The cubist image was structured to suggest the multiple perspectives by which we invest the object with properties of simultaneous meanings, properties that are descriptive of the actual transcript of our experience of the object. A well-known face seen in profile, for example,

93. Le Corbusier's Chapel at Ronchamp, 1950-55 *(Ezra Stoller, Photographs)*

is experienced in many ways as full-face; our experience of many different views of the face modifies what we see at a given moment and from a given angle, and so we are in a sense experiencing multiple perspectives.

The theory of multiple perspectives relates very closely to the organic theory of time. It is Whitehead's view that multiple perspectives, each with its individual way of involving itself in the world, are required during the accumulation of notions and feelings that constitute our response to the various sense cues of the object. Time, which is locked into the individual perspectives, thus enters into the concreteness of the object. Merleau-Ponty reminds us how we perceive an object. He uses the terms "grasp" and "take up" to describe our appropriation of various sense data or cues of an object. He treats time not as the linear link we make between the object and past events but as the network of *intentionalities* (Merleau-Ponty's word for perspectives) that we use in "grasping" and "taking up" the various aspects of the object. Experience is a continual merging and emerging of intentionalities, evolving out of many separate times and thus together referring to many "times." Merleau-Ponty denies the need for a synthesis aimed at signifying one single concrete time.[3]

While any object that we "take up" by perception is subject to a continual merging and emerging of perspectives, the great wall of Ronchamp (fig. 1) affords us an example in which unusually rich resources have been provided for a directed interplay. Among the

details of the wall are handmade rough textures, colored glass, and clear glass. Very important are the contrasts between narrowing slits and splayed, widening openings (fig. 94). As well as providing references to a variety of contrasting European archetypes of windows and walls, these forms involve the body in several contrasting tensions. Large openings, the height of a man, at floor level allow the body to "enter" physically into the wall and thus into history as well. With these accessible windows, Le Corbusier gives us a surprising vantage point and a fresh metaphor.

The attitude that would ignore the problem of time and the complexities of its expression is derived from classical philosophy and a science that visualized self-contained, unchanging entities and laws existing independent of time. Perhaps the most fundamental contrast between the organic view and the Cartesian can be expressed in terms of time conceived as a problem for expression. The organic view seeks to accommodate time. It seeks to devise modes of organization that will encourage the perception of the multiple perspectives that our experience generates from the object. When men have oriented themselves to building in ecologically sound ways and have worked through the quest for the technologically foolproof, I believe the dominant interest of architects will become the accommodation of time. The architects of great cathedrals achieved a high degree of accommodation by including earlier historical types of architecture and sculpture within the form of the cathedral. Ronchamp seems to involve time through a wider range of experiences, organized by insights suggested by recent discoveries in mathematics, physics, painting, and the psychology of perception.

Another side of the organic attitude, illustrated in some of the works of Frank Lloyd Wright, is the belief that there is something in the development of life that cannot be explained in physical terms alone. After an apprenticeship with Sullivan, Wright emerged as an exponent of the organic view. He conceived his buildings as models of natural organisms whose incipient characteristics respond to physical forces in the environment to produce purposeful growth and form. One must allow for forces other than the physical in Wright's work, however. He believed the most important of the characteristics of man to be his spiritual aspirations. These aspirations respond to the contingencies of time and place to produce architectural expressions as widely diverse as, for instance, the Mayan and the Gothic.

Wright seemed to have certain ideas in common with Whitehead, who, in his consideration of the extent to which the forms of nature may evolve, speculated on the possibility of the existence of beings able to weigh alternative values with some choices that lie outside of physical laws and are expressible only in terms of their own purpose.[4] Whitehead's speculation, best considered as an outgrowth of his theory of organic mechanism, suggests that evolution may be continued to levels of higher complexity through an agency

94. Le Corbusier's Chapel at Ronchamp *(Ezra Stoller, Photographs)*

that is not entirely explained by the observations of purely physical forces. While it is difficult to explain how the belief in such an agency can be objectified in an image, I believe that such an objectification is evident in much of Wright's architecture. There is an accumulative richness in such works as the Hanna house and the Unitarian church at Oak Park to which one can attribute a sense of spiritual direction. The harmony of many forces is insufficiently explained by sheer physical necessity. If one believes that the evolution of life on earth generally shows a trend toward higher complexity and sensitiveness, he may find a physical expression of the idea in the work of Wright; he may also find a model that encourages the harmonization of ever-widening contrasts.

Moreover, with Wright, the sheer statement of what things are, as in the revelation of the qualities of materials and the expression of architectural building types for particular situations, becomes an endeavor that places man in a dialogue with an evolutionary nature. Variety and organic fit are demanded in such an approach. The repetition of forms based on deterministic, mechanistic, and stylistic interpretations of man's architectural needs is ruled out by organic theory and by the suggestion of diversity in Wright's best architecture.

The organic theorist who has exerted perhaps the most important influence on my approach to architecture is Whitehead. Of particular importance for architecture is his notion that the body qualifies our experience in a very fundamental way. Whitehead envisions consciousness and thought as evolutionary outgrowths of the ultimate particles of matter that constitute the human body. Consequently, the potential for thought is in a sense inherent in the activities of these particles and their various arrangements in the body. And the functioning of the brain is conditioned by the antecedent functioning of other parts of the animal body. This view leads to the concept that our notions and feelings are bound up in the transmutation of sense data through bodily regions such as the organs for breathing, the eyes, the limbs, the systems that control our sense of physical balance, and so forth. In this way, thoughts are qualified by the bodily experience during the cognitive process.[5]

The experience of living in our bodies affects what we do, how we perceive, and how we react emotionally. In Whitehead's words, the older theory of sense perception accepts the "notion of mere receptive entertainment . . . which for no obvious reason, by reflection acquires an affective tone. The very opposite is the true explanation. The true doctrine of sense perception is that qualitative characters of affective tones inherent in bodily functionings are transmuted into the characters of [the shapes, colors, and arrangements of the objects we perceive]."[6]

The role of the body in perception, as propounded by Whitehead and Merleau-Ponty, seems to me to constitute the basis for a nearly revolutionary element in design. The functionalist, technologist, and stylist attitudes displayed in most modern architecture have ignored or only superficially recognized the correspondence between the body and the designed object. If designers are to be concerned with expressing the most significant realities of human experience, they cannot leave the expression of bodily experience to random intuitions of artist architects.

The bodily experience seems so pervasive and so inescapable that one may wonder whether an enlightened attitude that stresses bodily importance would have any effect on the designed environment. We must remember that we are habitually disposed to minimize bodily experience because we have learned Cartesian strategies for evaluating objects and buildings. Thus the environment of buildings in Western culture awaits the qualification of surface, mass, proportion, form, and space which will enable us to recognize the valued knowledge that only the body enables us to possess. Space and form derived from bodily experience will not imitate the appearance of the human body, but designed space and form will offer resources of texture, color, shape, and spatial arrangement derived from bodily experience, and this will encourage man to "take up" and possess his built environment. The interdependence between the physical and the cognitive will be dramatized.

Once we recognize that the body is the organism that regulates our cognizance of the world, we look for other means of determining values in our cognitive transactions with objects. If we admit with Whitehead that the psychological field, for all its complexity, is as real as any other natural occurrence, we can approach the problem of finding values in objects by adopting his theory of "prehensive unification," or the integration of separate sense data into a single image. This theory offers a rendering of what happens when we are cognizant of an object, as is explained in the brief discussion of the theory in section 16. The important point for designers is that if individual sense cues can elicit specific valued responses, the cues can be restructured in images so that concepts and feelings that are attached to the cues can be made to recur.

While it is admitted that the success of any man-made image depends upon its eliciting responses based on acquired experience, the organic attitude attempts to deal with valued experience of individuals and cultures on a conscious level. Thus the organic attitude in architecture expresses a concern for creating continuity and enhancing established values in the psychological life of the organism by consciously reconstituting in images cues to which significant experiences of individuals can be attached. At a time when man's use of industrialization and technology is ravaging established cultures and the natural environment as well, the maintenance and evolution of psychological identity would seem to be an issue of great importance. Images used in the environment can help maintain existing values as well as create evolutionary change.

In this book I have made distinctions between various attitudes and beliefs as they affect the design and interpretation of images.

In actual practice, distinctions between the organic attitude and what I have termed the Cartesian attitude are not always clear-cut, for forms that stem from seemingly opposed attitudes are often mingled. La Tourette (fig. 50), for example, responds both to the Cartesian and to the organic attitudes. The separation of the building from the site by pilotis and its self-contained, rectangular geometry relate to the Cartesian tradition. Its sensitivity to textures, its clear expression of materials, and its use of poetic metaphor show that La Tourette is at ease with the organic.

While I have criticized the Cartesian attitude because I believe it is based on erroneous assumptions about perception and experience, I also believe that symbols of Cartesian beliefs in images can evoke valued experiences for those who have absorbed the Cartesian tradition. It is to be remembered that disagreement with what a symbol stands for is not necessarily a reason for its deletion from an image. If known psychological values can be attributed to the symbol, it can be integrated with other components in the image. In La Tourette, Le Corbusier has given us an archetypally self-contained building set apart from the landscape. The idea of a self-contained entity that is independent of nature, though not consistent with an organic view of the world, has a long history in European thought, and values will probably be attached to the conception for a long time to come.

One inestimable value of images is that they allow us to become aware of changes in our attitudes and beliefs. La Tourette pro- vides a poignant example of an image representing a particular stage of European beliefs and attitudes. In this image we are made aware of Cartesian components, which dramatize the static and isolated, as well as of organic processes, which require interdependent relationships among diverse entities. It is a characteristic of the organic process in nature that features of forms undergoing evolution gradually change as they respond to new conditions in the environment. The image allows us to be aware of change and thus helps us perceive opportunities of changing or eliminating features of life which we hold to be faulty or outside our best interests. It is idle to speculate about whether Le Corbusier thought of this in designing La Tourette. But we can ponder the image as a composition that can help answer our psychological needs of establishing identity amid change.

We can hope that, as mankind becomes conscious of the process by which symbols put men in touch with the world and with himself, we can look forward to creating and controlling our environment in the light of knowledge that was not available to previous civilizations. But it remains to be seen whether even with such knowledge we can alter the current technological, economic, and social inertias which are obliterating the slowly evolved symbol systems of cultures and individuals. If the architecture of the future is to offer comfort and shelter in any complete sense it must keep as one of its conscious goals the satisfaction of man's psychological needs.

# NOTES

## 1

1. Wilder Penfield, "The Physiological Basis of the Mind," in *Control of the Mind*, ed. Seymour M. Farber and Roger Wilson (New York: McGraw-Hill, 1961), pp. 3-17.

2. It is the nature of an image to gather together into one conception the things its particular forms roughly fit. The roof of Ronchamp will be considered in some detail in later discussions because of the rich variety of references included in its single image.

3. Arthur Koestler, *The Act of Creation* (New York: Macmillan Co., 1964), p. 539 (italics added). Cf. Thomas A. Harris, *I'm OK—You're OK* (New York: Harper and Row, 1969), pp. 8-12.

4. Koestler, *Act of Creation*, p. 539 (italics added).

5. Ibid., p. 642.

## 3

1. Koestler gives an interesting analysis of the way the mind codifies experience and employs strategies to select and interpret the code. *The Act of Creation* (New York: Macmillan Co., 1964), pp. 38-45.

2. The intent of the advertising artists who airbrush images of genitals into the ice cubes in advertisements for the liquor industry is discussed in Brian Wilson Key's *Subliminal Seduction* (Englewood Cliffs, N.J.: Prentice-Hall, 1973). This book offers substantiation on a pragmatic level of the theory that images are picked up by the subconscious mind and can influence behavior.

3. In Gestalt terminology a matrix is analogous to a closure of meaning. The concepts of matrix, code, and strategy apply to the image as a whole and also to its details. During the dialectical interaction between the beholder and the image, matrices affecting both details and the whole may be governed by more than one code. The dialectic process is described in the next section.

It is both accurate and helpful to treat the whole image as subject to a single matrix or closure, but it is equally accurate and important to think of the whole as being continually subject to intrusion by the codes governing the details. If one is content to simplify a complex image by confining it within a neat verbal description of a single closure, vital ingredients supplied by the details may be overlooked.

4. Curiously the initial reaction of several students in different seminars has been a startled laugh or near-laugh. Among conjectured reasons for this response: it is a reflex action that mimics the tension lines of the mouth, mixed with confusion caused by momentary misreading of *cry* and *laugh* and a subconscious relief that another is engaged in a tragic experience and not oneself.

## 4

1. Arthur Koestler, *The Act of Creation* (New York: Macmillan Co., 1964), p. 533.

2. Alfred North Whitehead, *Process and Reality* (New York: Macmillan Co., 1929), p. 472.

3. Ibid., p. 472.

4. Heinrich Zimmer, *The Art of Indian Asia* (New York: Pantheon Books, 1955), p. 90.

5. "The unity of a work of art stems primarily from the interdependence of its elements, and is further secured by this dialectical pattern of their relations. The dialectic is a phase principle; the consummation of one phase is the preparation for another." Susanne K. Langer, *Mind: An Essay on Human Feeling* (Baltimore, Md.: Johns Hopkins Press, 1967), pp. 204-6.

**5**

1. Rudolph Arnheim, *Visual Thinking* (Berkeley: University of California Press, 1971), p. 170.

2. One may feel that a sort of stupidity is projected by the Mayan head, but this feeling is usually sublimated by other, more dominant feelings. The flexible strategies of lip codes allow for sentience instead of stupidity.

3. The response of the viewer is akin to the awareness of two or more planes of experience at once, as described in the section on timelessness.

**6**

1. Sir Nikolaus Pevsner, *An Outline of European Architecture* (Harmondsworth, Middlesex: Penguin Books, 1943), p. 122.

2. Nervi's views appear in detail in his *Structures* (New York: F. W. Dodge, 1956).

3. By bodily feelings I mean our reactions to scale, our sense of balance, and the tactile and other sensations provoked by the experience of our bodies.

**7**

1. Bergson was among the first to formulate a concept of images expressive of this idea. "Diverse images borrowed from different orders of things can, by the convergency of their action, direct consciousness to a point where there is an intuition to be seized." *An Introduction to Metaphysics*, tr. T. E. Hime (New York: Bobbs Merrill, 1955), p. 27.

2. Time is to be considered in the modern manner as inseparable from space. In this sense a reference to time is also a reference to space.

**8**

1. Amos Rapoport and Robert E. Kantor, "Complexity and Ambiguity in Environmental Design," *Journal of the American Institute of Planners* 33(July 1967):210-21.

2. Ibid.

**10**

1. The term *existential* refers here to the phenomenological perspective of one's lived experience. Elements of such experience include one's knowledge of the world gained through the senses, expression of the self through bodily action and gesture, and awareness of one's private attitudes and sensitivities.

2. Maurice Merleau-Ponty, *The Phenomenology of Perception*, tr. Colin Smith (New York: Humanities Press, 1962), p. 305.

3. Form archetypes for a house are likely to be different from those of a school or bank.

4. Sir Kenneth Clark, *Civilisation* (New York: Harper and Row, 1969), p. 266.

**11**

1. Ludwig von Bertalanffy, as paraphrased by Edgar J. Kaufmann, Jr., in "The Usonian Pope-Leighey House," *Historic Preservation* 21(April-September 1969):119.

2. Sean Jennet, "Britannia Deserta," *Landscape* 15(1965):22-29.

**13**

1. The shingled form is aggressive in the illustration, but when approached frontally by the access drive it is open and welcoming.

2. Louis Kahn, *The Spirit of Architecture* (New York: American Iron and Steel Institute, 1950).

**14**

1. Susanne K. Langer, *Mind: An Essay on Human*

*Feeling* (Baltimore, Md.: Johns Hopkins Press, 1967), pp. 62-64.

2. A potent means of differentiating stored experience that may pertain to an image is to examine the root meanings of the word that names it. For instance, the word *window* stems from the Old Norse *vindauga*, a compound of *vind(r)* (wind or air) and *auga* (eye). The window of the Prairie House is rather like an eye looking out at the world. The root of *wind* or *air* can be recalled by the hooded overhang and the minimally visible glass setting that contributes to the ambiguity between exterior and interior. The irregular appearance of shingles and boards may also contribute to notions of wind and air. I believe that allusions to the roots of the word were implicit, although unconscious, in the design process of the window.

3. Eero Saarinen, *Challenge to an Architect* (Moline, Ill.: Deere and Company Administrative Center, 1964), p. 35.

## 15

1. Edmund Burke Feldman, *Art as Image and Idea* (Englewood Cliffs, N.J.: Prentice-Hall, 1967), pp. 472-73.

2. René Dubos, *So Human an Animal* (New York: Scribners, 1961), pp. 158-59.

3. Alfred North Whitehead, *An Enquiry concerning the Principles of Natural Knowledge* (London: Cambridge University Press, 1955), pp. 196-97.

## 16

1. Arthur Koestler, *The Act of Creation* (New York: Macmillan Co., 1964), p. 208.

2. Another motivation that can be traced to this student project is the attempt to create the illusion of mass or bulk without the appearance of weight. Influenced by the dynamics of Wright's house for Edgar Kaufmann and by recent scientific notions concerning gravity, mass, and energy, I qualified the sloping walls of the post office and its roof with changing profiles that are like asymptotes expressing an ambiguous fluctuation between the appearance of mass and its disappearance. A similar intention can be seen in the shaping of the asymmetrical ellipse of the Prairie House plan and in the patterns of its wood siding (frontispiece, figs. 13, 14).

3. William James, quoted in Ralph Barton Perry, *The Thought and Character of William James* (New York: George Braziller, 1954), p. 275.

4. Alfred North Whitehead, *Science and the Modern World* (London: Cambridge University Press, 1932), pp. 86-92, 156-58; and *Process and Reality* (New York: Macmillan Co., 1929), pp. 95-197.

## 18

1. "The Time House," *Architectural Design* 38 (1968):249.

2. N. J. Habraken, *Supports* (New York: Praeger, 1972).

## 19

1. John Dewey, *Art as Experience* (New York: Capricorn, 1934), p. 220; David Denton, *The Language of Ordinary Experience* (New York: Philosophical Library, 1970), p. 47.

2. Martin Pawley, *Architecture versus Housing* (New York: Praeger, 1971), p. 97.

3. American slang offers an example, particularly when an American term like *beatnik* or *hippie* is compared with the British *Teddy boy* or *angry young man*. The *nik* in *beatnik* suggests the Russian-Yiddish context popularized in the comic strips of Al Capp and reminds us of the Russian *Nyet* of the postwar UN debates. This suffix acts as a negative, yet humorous, qualification and as a signal of long hair and beards. *Beat*, of course, is a signal of

defeat, lassitude, and the rejection of establishment values projected by a postwar generation. The British *Teddy boy* is not a compression into one word; it thus lacks the "plucked out of diversity" feeling of the American terms. And *angry young man* spells out literal meaning instead of abstracting and compressing meaning as the American term *beatnik* does.

4. Margaret J. Drury, *Mobile Homes: The Unrecognized Revolution in American Housing* (New York: Praeger, 1972), p. 11.

## 20

1. Vincent Scully describes two recurring psychological drives in Americans. One is the nomadic urge, a product of open horizons and impatience with communal restraints. The other is the impulse to establish deep roots in the earth. Much of the housing designed by Frank Lloyd Wright can be seen to objectify both of these characteristics in one poetic image. His own home in the desert near Phoenix, Arizona, is a striking example. A tent of canvas stretched between redwood frames spans massive concrete and masonry wall forms. The tent suggests the transitory while the heavy, battered walls suggest an earthbound permanence. The courtyard framework likewise accommodates both change and permanence.

2. A fascinating view of this phenomenon is to be found in Studs Terkel, *Working* (New York: Pantheon Books, 1972).

3. Ian McHarg, *Design with Nature* (New York: Doubleday & Co., 1969), p. 20.

4. Frances Yates, *The Art of Memory* (Chicago: University of Chicago Press, 1966), pp. 2-7.

## 21

1. *Process and Reality* (New York: Macmillan Co., 1929).

2. Also ignored was the polychromy of Greek and Roman architecture, which was known through archeological investigations as early as the eighteenth century.

3. "A Summation of Parts," *Progressive Architecture* (June 1972):82.

## 22

1. Erich Kahler, *The Disintegration of Form in the Arts* (New York: Braziller, 1968), p. 80.

## 23

1. Gertrude Stein, "Composition as Explanation," in her *What Are Masterpieces* (Los Angeles: Conference Press, 1940), pp. 23-28.

2. Alfred North Whitehead, *Science and the Modern World* (London: Cambridge University Press, 1932), p. 70.

## 24

1. Henry James, *The Art of Fiction* in *Representative Selections*, Lyon N. Richardson, ed. (New York: American Book Co., 1941), p. 86; Louis Sullivan, *A System of Architectural Ornament* (New York: Press of the American Institute of Architects, 1924).

2. The importance of collage is alluded to in section 3, particularly in the references to Koestler's concept of bisociation. Eisenstein points out that collage has been a powerful device in art throughout history and sees it as the basis of dialectic in the arts.

3. Merleau-Ponty, *The Phenomenology of Perception* (New York: Humanities Press, 1962), pp. 69, 239-42, 410-33.

4. Alfred North Whitehead, *Science and the Modern World* (London: Cambridge University Press, 1932), p. 134.

5. It is interesting that phenomenologists have come to conclusions similar to those of Whitehead.

Merleau-Ponty explores the problems of how the body affects perception. He describes the body as an object sensitive to all other objects before it. The body prepares itself for whatever object it encounters, whether the object be sound, word, or visual form. "The body, insofar as it has 'behavior patterns' is the object which uses its own parts as a general system of symbols for the world and through which we can consequently 'be at home in' that world, 'understand it' and find significance in it." *The Phenomenology of Perception*, tr. Colin Smith (New York: Humanities Press, 1962), p. 236.

6. Alfred North Whitehead, *Adventures of Ideas* (New York: Macmillan Co., 1956), p. 276.

# INDEX

Cunningham house, 138, 154-58, figs. 77-79

Daniel, Mann, Johnson: office building, 183-84, fig. 91
DeLuca residence project (Greene), 94, 95, 153-54, figs. 45, 46
Denton, David, 147
Descartes, René, 10, 178-79; theory of perception of, 178
Designer's objects as form determinants, 137-41
*Design with Nature* (McHarg), 168
Dewey, John, 147
Dialectic, 21-22, 43, 65, 201 n. 5
Dialogue: among rhythms, 124; between designer and user, 149
*Dialogues* (Whitehead), 193
Diamond and Myers: Galleria Housing Union Building, 106-7, fig. 61
*Dora Maar* (Picasso), 61-62, fig. 28
Dubos, René, 121-22; *So Human an Animal*, 37
Duchamp, Marcel, 127-28, 189

Eiffel Tower, 10
Eisenstein, Sergei Mikhailovich, 9, 204 n. 1; *Film Form,* 17
Elrod house (Lautner), 88-89, fig. 40
*Enquête sur l'évolution littèraire* (Mallarmé), 53
Entrances, 101-5
*Ère du soupçon, L'* (Sarraute), 189
Existential awareness: defined, 202 n. 1; merged with cultural awareness, 43; of time, 49

Falling Water (Wright), 119-20, 203 n. 2
Feelings objectified in images, 18-19, 23-35, 58-59; and Cartesianism, 192; existential, 43; by geometric forms, 18, 29-30; by proportions, 20-21
Feldman, Edmund Burke: *Art as Image and Idea*, 189
Field: and collection of fragments, 65; and figure composition, 61-62; perceptual, 22; and sculptural events of Cunningham house, 157-58
Figure-ground composition, 81
*Film Form* (Eisenstein), 17
Financing of housing, 162-63; as form determinant, 145

*Four Saints in Three Acts* (Stein), 66
Frame of reference. *See* Matrix
French house (Greene), 96-98, 139, 141, figs. 47-49
Frozen time: in Vermeer works, 49, 63
Furchess residence (Greene), 103-4, figs. 53, 54
Furniture. *See* User's objects as form determinants

Galleria Housing Union Building (Diamond and Myers), 106-7
Gandhi, Mohandas Karamchand, 33, fig. 18
Gaudí, Antonio, 75; Colonia Güell Chapel, 125, fig. 70; Park Güell, 125
Geometric forms, 26, 30, 32, 118, 134-35; as Cartesian heritage, 177, 179, 182; and feelings, 18, 29-30; in pop architecture, 190-91
Gestalt psychology, 62, 201 n. 3
Gesture, 26; in architecture, 92, 119-20, 156-57; as model, 61
Getty tomb (Sullivan), 71, 131, fig. 32
*Girl in a Red Hat* (Vermeer), 25-26, 49, 58, fig. 10
Goethe, Johann Wolfgang von: *Conversations with Eckerman*, 7
Goff, Bruce, xii, 75; grain bin house, 191, fig. 92
Goodhue, Bertram, 87
Grain bin house (Goff), 121, fig. 92
Gropius, Walter, 182

Habraken, N. J., 144; *Supports*, 147
Hanna house (Wright), 198
"Happenings," 186, 188
Harmonies, defined, 111-12
High-rise: buildings, 173-76; project (Greene), 174-76, figs. 86, 87
Hindu figure from Khajuraho, 32, fig. 17
*House, Form, and Culture* (Rapoport), 93
Howard Johnson restaurants, design of, 159
*Human Condition, The* (Arendt), 161
Human purposes revealed in architecture, 40
Human scale, 29, 81, 97-98, 145; function of, 117-18; in Mayan architecture, 42, 117-18; in Wright's buildings, 118-19

Hume, David, 178
Hurtig, John: drawing, 26-27, 128, fig. 12

Idealized patterns in art images, 51-52
"Ideals" as defined by Rapoport and Kantor, 58
Images: applied as styling, 159; based on life experiences, xi, xii, 16, 99-107; based on machines and technology, xii, 41, 176, 177, 180, 187-88; components of, xi, 10, 20; cues and contexts in, 7, 10, 13, 14-16, 20, 24-26; defined, xi, xii, 43; feelings projected into, 23, 26-36, 58; functions of, xiii, 1, 2, 5, 26, 36, 37, 41, 43, 51, 58; and idealized patterns, 51; incorporating real objects, 44; and models, 61-66; objectifying valued concepts and feelings, 27; timeless, 47; valued, 24, 49
"Independent existence," 178
International Style, 179

James, Henry, and organic theory, 193, 194
James, William, and organic theory, 132, 193
*Jesus Christ Superstar*: and caricature, 22; and dialectic, 22, 65; merges bodily feelings with traditional beliefs, 43
*Jewish Bride* (Rembrandt), 62
John Deere Headquarters (Saarinen), 114-15, fig. 64
Johnson Wax Building (Wright), fig. 31; and texture, 69-70
Joyce house (Greene), figs. 55-58; design synthesis of, 132-35, 138, 141, 194; entrance to, 104-5; and figure-ground composition, 81; metaphor in, 113, 130

Kahn, Louis, 147; on windows, 105
Kantor, Robert E., 55-56, 58
Kaufmann, Edgar, 119
Kennedy, John F., 35, 44, fig. 19
Key, Brian Wilson: *Subliminal Seduction,* 201 n. 2
Knowledge-feeling response, 37, 51
Koestler, Arthur, 15; *The Act of Creation*, 7, 11, 47; on matrices, 13, 201

209